REAL LEADERS FOR THE REAL WORLD

Essential Traits of Successful
and Authentic Leaders

John McLachlan & Karen Meager

Real Leaders for the Real World

First published in 2014 by

Panoma Press
48 St Vincent Drive, St Albans, Herts, AL1 5SJ, UK

info@panomapress.com
www.panomapress.com

Book layout by Neil Coe.
Photography by Vicki Bunn Photography.

Printed on acid-free paper from managed forests.

ISBN 978-1-909623-56-9

Acknowledgements

We want to acknowledge the influence, impact and support of our former business colleagues, academic trainers, friends, students and clients. You have all been and continue to be our teachers.

Karen and John

Approved Testimonials for
Real Leaders for the Real World

"Better to have tried and failed than never to have tried at all."

**Martin Gilbert; Chief Executive,
Aberdeen Asset Management**

"So relevant. This book brings grounded scientific and psychological knowledge and real experience into a practical guide no leader should be without."

**Dr Wyatt Woodsmall PhD;
President of Advanced Behavioral Modeling Inc.**

"The concept of leadership is too often solely associated with those at the head of organisations. Leadership is a skill that all of us should hone. This is a great read. It explains quite complex topics in a way that the reader will get and learn from."

**Colin Kennedy; Senior Director,
Thomson Reuters Elite**

Contents

Introduction

The world needs more leaders. The world doesn't need more robots.

We are in a tricky place right now; the world is more diverse and complex than ever. With the spread of and access to information faster and broader than ever, gone are the days when people just do as they're told. For every fact there is a counter-argument, for every right way there are problems and complications. My way or the highway just doesn't cut it as a way to run a family, a business or a country.

The problem is that as a society, we haven't done a very good job in nurturing the next generation of leaders, because what is required is what most of us just don't have. There are few good examples to follow, which is not because the leaders we have are bad people, but because the whole realm of leadership is often seen as some mysterious arena, where only strong, fearless, special people live. Countless leadership books seem to support this.

Yet our experience working with leaders for many years has taught us that people who have the title Leader or are in a place of authority have the same problems and issues as the rest of us. Many are plagued with self-doubt, conflicting priorities and communication difficulties. These are common problems and ultimately possible to overcome and our aim in this book is to show you how to do just that and become a leader who is real.

This book will provide a pragmatic, practical development approach for people who are already leaders and want to lead in an authentic way, become more successful and do all of this with ease and grace. We are also looking to inspire people who do not see themselves as natural leaders, either because of their own self-doubt or because they look at what they think a leader is or the common perception of leadership as something 'only for the chosen few'.

Everyone has the potential for leading; there is no one formula for the 'perfect leader'. In this book we will show you how you can develop your own style as a leader, live the life you want to live and use your skills and abilities for good.

As part of writing this book, we have completed research with over 60 leaders from all walks of life, mainly business, and also public sector, community leaders and leaders of charities and families. In this book we will present the key factors for leaders' success as a result of this research and we will take you through how you too can develop yourself as a leader; no magic formula, no need to be someone you are not. You can be yourself and be a leader – fact.

Not everyone has the will or the capabilities to become a big leader in the business world. Not everyone wants to be the next Steve Jobs, Richard Branson or Barack Obama. Most people want to live a happy, fulfilled life though, and most people want to do a good job – whatever their area of interest or skill. So whether you run a multi-million pound business or want to lead your family in a way that nurtures everybody for success, this book will help you to identify your areas of self-development, train yourself to bring out the best in you and be a guiding light for others to follow.

Our research has shown that there are some key things good leaders do well, even if they all do them differently and with their own style. It is simple – yes, and achieving them is in the pile of 'easier said than done'. Relax though, with our help and armed with the knowledge and practical tips in this book, it is very achievable for most people – very achievable.

In this book we will take you through each of these elements, outline why they are not naturally developed in people and why this is a problem. We will then help you to identify where you are, where you want to be and give you some easy-to-follow steps to get there.

We have been there, done it and are working on the T-shirt. Our background is in business leadership so we know what it's like to be there and the real problems that leaders face. We know that theory is interesting and often hard to apply in the real world. Since starting Monkey Puzzle many years ago, we have developed our psychological knowledge, and putting this together with our business (and human) experience, we have supported many people to become the true leaders they are. We are not interested in developing clones of ourselves; we are most definitely not perfect. We are constantly inspired by how people can find better, more creative and more exciting solutions for themselves than we can give them. We are experts in taking complex applied psychology and science and applying this to real people in the real world to solve their problems and achieve their goals and dreams. In this book we have integrated knowledge from experts in their field and link it to practical, actionable steps that you can take to be the leader you want to be.

We want to see leaders out there in the world who are unique in their personality and style, doing good work and making the world a better place.

PART 1

THE FOUNDATIONS OF REAL LEADERS

CHAPTER 1

Why we need Real Leaders in the Real World

"The three most important jobs on this planet are Parents, Teachers and Leaders."

Frank Pucelik

Leader. Now there's a word that can generate a strong reaction in most of us, and lead to arguments around any dinner table or post-work pub get-together. What makes a good leader, what makes a bad one? Does the world need leaders who are strong, single-minded and driven to get things done quickly, or leaders that are flexible, able to listen to everyone's opinions and who take time to reflect and consider before doing anything?

We suspect your answer will be a reflection of what you believe, how you have been brought up and your experience of leadership up to this point. If you look around you, you will see many examples of leaders –

some good, some not so good. Our judgment of a good or bad leader will be dependent on our point of view, it has to be. To evaluate anything, we need to process it in our own head, connect it up with what we already understand or our life experience. That makes it subjective; it makes it our point of view. As the rational, intelligent people we think we are, we will, of course, have many facts, statistics and evidence that will clearly demonstrate that our point of view is correct. It's what keeps us sane, safe and secure in our world – knowing we are right and being able to justify it.

The reason there is so much argument and discussion about good leaders is that what makes a good leader is, like most things, based on our opinion.

Think about someone you think is a good leader. Why do you think they are a good leader? We all focus on different aspects of a person's behaviours based on our own beliefs and values, our own aspirations and our own limitations.

Let's consider a few recent prominent leaders in the world.

For those of you from the UK of a certain age, Margaret Thatcher evokes strong emotions, depending on what your (or more often, what your parents') political persuasion was, where you lived at the time and what your parents did for a living. When she died, we were shocked by the outpouring of emotions that the passing of an elderly woman who had not been in power for a generation gave rise to. The polarisation of a nation was clear, with those whose obvious and deep rage against all that she stood for was matched by the feelings of genuine admiration shown by an equal number of people.

The thing is, whether she was or wasn't a great leader depends on your values, your attitudes and your perception of the results of her time in charge of this country. We've read many books about her and there is very little everyone can agree on, as whether she was a great leader or not depends on your opinion and memory and less on facts. With the passing of time, both those who supported her and those who didn't can still argue about the impact she had on the world.

Now look to the other side of the Atlantic and arguably the current most recognisable leader in the world – no, not Homer Simpson, we mean Barack Obama. Another leader who divides opinion based on your values and beliefs. For some he is a strong, quiet, self-assured, diplomatic, long-term focused leader who has the capacity to see all sides, reflect and take decisions for the greater good. To others he is a dithering, weak, indecisive leader who changes his mind weekly and is style over substance. How you view him will depend on which qualities you focus on, your attitude to time (long-term/short-term) and your own beliefs and values. His behaviours, decisions and actions can be interpreted in many different ways. This is true of all leaders, and true of all of us.

> ## Myth Buster - Objectivity
>
> There is no such thing as an objective view, there are only degrees of subjectivity. The minute we take something inside ourselves, we make it subjective and it is influenced by our own feelings, experiences, beliefs and values. Having more data than someone else about a topic or having more people who agree with you does not make it objective, it just makes it acceptable to more people. We spend our life looking to get people to agree with our opinion.

We need Leaders

" In democracy we get the government we deserve."

French political philosopher Alexis de Tocqueville

All of this would be interesting and not very important if it weren't for the fact that our leaders are shaping the future of our world. They run our families, our communities, our businesses and our countries and we need them.

Parents, teachers and leaders are the most important jobs on this planet. Within these three roles our next generations will be nurtured, developed and educated. Their relationships with those around them, their environment, community and wider world will be guided by the leaders they come into contact with. Their behaviour in the workplace, self-esteem and mental health will all be shaped by their leaders – that is you and me and the political and business leaders we elect and support.

There's a lot at stake.

The problem is that, as it stands at present, this responsibility is being left to a chosen few, chosen not by their skills, qualities or fitness for the job, but chosen by luck, timing, desire to be a leader, upbringing or position in life. This cannot be the future.

Too many of our leaders today, whether it be in the family, community, politics or business, do not have the emotional stability, level of integrity and expansive thinking required to do the job that we need them to do now and in the future. You only have to read the newspapers, watch television or be an employee in many organisations to see that those who are supposedly leading us are not up to the job.

This is not to cast judgment over our current leaders so that we can feel smug and righteous about it from our dining room tables. Let's be clear, being a good leader is very much easier said than done. This is why so many books are written on leadership and yet it is difficult to find a good example of leadership we can all agree on.

"We choose the go to the moon in this decade and do the other things. Not because they are easy, because they are hard,"

John F. Kennedy

Yes, you could follow the current and easy path of promotion into leadership in your career by doing what is familiar and acceptable and apparently successful in your workplace culture. You could lead your family by the accepted and familiar rules that you grew up with and that are socially acceptable. You could run for office by aligning with this party or that party and spend your time negating and criticising the other side to gain popularity and election. You could.

Yet how many people do you know who follow this path and are unfulfilled? How many leaders do you hear speak and you say "I don't believe what they are saying"? We see it too in the work that we do with many talented people who are restricting themselves and their potential to conform to a stereotype rather than be themselves.

This is the path that so many people follow; even though they might not feel fulfilled and rewarded by it, it is the easier route, the acceptable route. The harder and ultimately more fulfilling route is to be yourself, and that takes courage, commitment and self-awareness.

So all the competency matrices in the world will not a good leader make. Personality profiling tools are useful, up to a point, and having leadership development programmes that teach some general skills are helpful. What makes a good leader, though, is not a formulaic, tick-box exercise. It will never be possible for us all to agree that 'so-and-so' is a great leader, that all great leaders should look like this, have this level of education, speak in a certain way. What we are saying is that when it comes to leadership, the nurturing of the next generation and the growth of the world we live in, each and every one of us has our part to play, that leaders come in many shapes and sizes and we believe, strongly as you can probably tell, that the key to great leadership is not in a list of skills that a leader must acquire. Leadership is in the development of the person themselves, their emotional regulation, their integrity and in their ability for expansive thinking. These traits are the foundation upon which any skills can sit and be fully, effectively and efficiently utilised. This is different for each and every one of us and that is both the challenge and the opportunity that we are asking you to sign up for. We can all play our part.

Are we saying that we need more leaders or better leaders? Yes to both.

This book is aimed at you if you are aspiring to be a leader or do not think you are a leader but have the nurture, development and education of our future generations at heart. This book is also for you if you are already a leader and have the awareness, desire and passion to be the best leader you can be in your own way and in your own style.

In our work we support existing leaders to do just this and help non-leaders develop themselves, their self-esteem and their own style to step into their own brand of leadership. This has included leaders of business, charities, families and, dare we say it, leaders in their own lives.

Leadership is no longer for the select few, it is for the many. You can do it too, we will show you how in this book.

So whether you want to be the leader of the best quality business in your area of interest, create the most cohesive, energetic, innovative team or be an award-winning entrepreneur and philanthropist, we want to help you.

What is Leadership?

Throughout history, leadership has always been important and revered. Think of your own favourite tale of great leadership. Was it Churchill 'fighting on the beaches'; Boudicca standing up for her beliefs and paying the ultimate price; or Martin Luther King with his dream? Who is your idea of a leader and what is it about them that inspires you?

The thing about the tales of great leaders is that they are inspirational, they suggest qualities that no one else has. They imply that only the chosen few will be great leaders and that the skills to do it are rare, given to you at birth and your destiny.

Think Luke Skywalker in the *Star Wars* films. Given who his father was, there was little doubt he was the chosen one!

As any good history teacher will tell you, the other thing about history is that there are very few absolute facts. Stories are presented to suit the time and they are rarely the complete picture. Churchill was renowned as a brilliant wartime leader but did not do so well in peacetime. Was Henry VIII a tyrant or a leader of his time? On a recent visit to Warwick Castle, we had the pleasure of watching Henry VIII 'on trial'. As the actors played out the roles for and against the king, it unfolded that there was a great deal of myth and historical rewriting in the history books that saw him as a womanising, self-centred, spoilt brat. There is another side. There is always another side.

Historical leaders are all 'of their time'; what we needed in the world in times past when we were landing on beaches and conquering is not what we need now. This may still be happening, but it is not happening in the same way, on the same scale and we need different leaders and more – many, many more – of them to take our world forward. The future of the world is dependent on our embracing difference, expanding our thinking and moving away from the polarised thinking of the past.

Whilst the world is getting smaller in terms of travel and communication, it is getting bigger in terms of opportunities and challenges. Even 50 years ago we were less concerned about the world outside our country, even our village. Now the future of the planet is dependent on us all doing our bit.

It's no longer big governments and big organisations who have the ability, structural size and capability to make an impact in the world. With the amazing speed of technological development, the worldwide web, smart phones, Wi-Fi, and the explosion of social media, and more and more ways to connect with people, anyone can make an impact in the world and more of us need to. Even one person can be the leader in their niche. Countless YouTube phenomena are testimony to this.

Definition of Leadership (for what it's worth)

There are hundreds of leadership books, courses on how to be the best leader, leadership coaches and so on. Yet what is a leader? Is there a set of criteria that equals a good leader, is it skills, is it personality, is it something you are born with or develop?

Looking at a range of dictionary definitions begins to show the issue we are up against as:

Oxford English	The person who leads or commands a group, organization, or country.
Dictionary.com	A person or thing that leads A guiding or directing head A person who guides

Well, that is all very helpful in stating the obvious. So let's try something else. What do the dictionaries say about the synonyms for leader?

Synonyms for Leader
Boss, captain, chief, commander, conductor, counsellor, director, doyen, eminence, forerunner, general, governor, guide, head, luminary, manager, pilot, pioneer, shepherd, superior.

So as you can see from the synonyms, there are lots of different types of leaders, and you can already recognise that the skills required to be a commander are different from those of a counsellor, as the skills of a pioneer differ from those of a manager, or a director from a shepherd.

And to be a leader you need followers, people who will follow you. To be a leader does not require clones, fans or groupies, servants, worshippers, minions, dependents. To be a leader requires that people will follow you because you can inspire them, they can believe in you, they trust you. Whilst it still exists in families, communities, business and countries, the days of the bullying leader are numbered, thankfully. People have much more mobility than before, more self-reliance, more opportunity and access to difference and they are less and less inclined to put up with poor leaders.

Formulaic Leadership

You may know leaders (you may even be one of them) who sound like they have swallowed one of those 'this is what you say, do and need to appear as to be a leader' kinds of books. They will use buzzwords that make no sense (and most are not even English), they are smokescreens on smokescreens; remember: 'it's a jungle out there' and 'we need to maximise the on-boarding of our staff'!

These are leaders who, when in doubt, ask for more and more information and like to use long words or TLAs (that's Three Letter Abbreviations to you and me) or if you're really stuck ETLAs (Extended Three Letter Abbreviations). We might have gone a little far here – but you get the point. And let's be clear, we're not saying we haven't done some of these ourselves. We have been in leadership positions, we've followed the management-speak handbook whilst inside screaming 'This is just rubbish'. We both shudder as we write this at the thought of some of the things we have said and done. What were we thinking? More importantly, what on earth were we saying?!

In our work with leaders we have helped them unpick and unpack all of this nonsense, become their authentic selves and become Real Leaders in the Real World.

In this book we are asking you to think about what kind of leader you are and give you the tools and ideas to develop your style, the style that fits you.

What is Real? (well not a lot actually)

We've already said that we all see things differently; from there it's not a seismic leap to 'we all have a different view of reality'.

We know many people, and are sure you do too, who like to tell you that they are 'just being honest' or 'just telling it like it is'. That may well be true, the bit that's missing from each of these opinion statements is 'for me' or 'as I see it'.

We all construct our own reality, so in this book when we talk about real we mean real for you, your reality. We want you to be yourself not a caricature of yourself or a robot following someone else's accepted idea of a leader.

When you are real, when you are yourself, life is clearer, more straightforward and less stressful. You don't have to put on a show, create an image or be fake. When you are being yourself, people will see that, they will believe that you believe what you are saying whether they agree with it or not. Believability is the basis of trust and with trust you can lead. The opposite is also true. Without trust you need to control and manipulate, you have to play games, create good guys and bad guys, them and us. This takes energy, creates stress and is ultimately unsuccessful.

"Sincerity: if you can fake it, you've got it made."

Daniel Schorr

You can't fake this – people know at some level even if they don't know exactly what it is they are reacting to. It's why someone can stand up at a conference, in a meeting, over dinner and say all the right words and you just don't buy it. It's why there are some people in whose company you do not feel comfortable, even though you can't put your finger on it. Don't let that person be you.

We all know that sometimes life is complex, that often there are not five steps to... a perfect solution, life, business, relationship. That's not to say it's not tempting. We're tempted by all the articles and books around the five steps to this, follow this and you'll be thin and how to be a millionaire by a week next Tuesday. They are attractive because we all like the thought of instant gratification and that life is a process, a series of steps that take us from A to B. Life isn't like that and we are not like that.

We are human beings, not robots, we are not logical. You may believe that you are logical and pride yourself on it, but trust us, you're not. You are a human being full of contradictions, fears, worries, as well as being full of potential, amazing strengths and skills and an infinite capacity to learn and grow. We are all like that. If you are unaware of the feelings that drive you, it's just that it's out of your conscious awareness. Our emotions are biologically designed to be internal information that helps us to make decisions and respond automatically and appropriately. Think about the word emotion, there is motion and movement in there. That's what makes us fantastic human beings (and why other people who are not as perfect and logical as us annoy us so much!).

So, we won't be able to resolve all of the issues of the world for you in the book, tempting as it may be to say we can. What we will give you is a way to be able to resolve some of them for yourself, the ones that are important to you, in a way that works for you.

Leadership Research

We conducted a study of over 60 leaders from various walks of life who either considered themselves 'a good leader' or were nominated to complete the research by someone else who saw them as 'a good leader'. We deliberately left the decision about what a good leader was to the individual. We didn't want to define what 'a good leader' was, this isn't important (and who are we to say?). We were interested in people's perceptions of a good leader. Our leadership research participants were:

- 48% male, 52% female
- 36% had children living at home
- 70% were aged between 40 and 60
- 67% were business leaders, 15% public sector, and the rest were a combination of family, community organisations, charities, sports and other leaders

The purpose of the study was to identify what good leaders have in common, what aspects of their leadership they find challenging and what is important to them. When we began reviewing the responses we were struck by the common themes that came out despite the differences in the people completing the study.

In our leadership research we wanted to discover different people's reality around leadership and identify the issues and problems that are part of that reality for them.

The overwhelming message in the study was that there is a common set of problems and challenges good leaders face and there is a set of key traits that good leaders either have or are striving to acquire.

We have used the results of the study to shape this book so that it addresses:

- The challenges leaders face in the real world and how you can overcome them.
- The common traits good leaders have and how you can develop your own.
- The personal development needs and desires of good leaders and how you can address them.

Throughout the book we will show you how to become emotionally regulated, what you can do to develop your expansive thinking and maintain your integrity in whatever way reflects and supports you best.

In Chapter 2 we will talk in detail about emotional regulation as it is a key aspect of becoming a successful leader and most definitely in the 'easier said than done' pile.

Part 2 - Real Leaders, Real Problems

In Part 2 we will consider the common problems and challenges highlighted by the participants in our study, those potentially unresolvable dilemmas of life. We will look at the degree to which they are unresolvable; should we simply accept these problems as a fact of life for example? We will also explore and explain some of the ways in which you can begin to manage and even overcome these problems and challenges in your life and work.

Real Leaders in the Real World find two main areas of life challenging.

The first is work/life balance and time in general. Whilst some of the leaders in our study found the balance between work and other areas of their life flowed well most of the time, a lot of the comments in the study reflected that a lot of participants found this area a constant juggling act.

In Chapter 3 we will look at the Age Old Problem of Time exploring the problems that inevitably arise and were confirmed by our study. We'll look at and help you to understand how your beliefs impact your ability to make the most of the time we all have available. We will also consider how the most effective leaders look at time and provide some practical steps you can take immediately to feel more in control of your time.

Like most of us in life, the second area leaders in our survey found challenging was dealing with difficult behaviours and certain types of people they come across in their lives and role as a leader.

In Chapter 4 we will dive into the murky world of other people and their impact on us. Most of us would like to think we are reasonable, considerate people yet there are just some people who rub us up the wrong way, behaviours that just hit our buttons and people we find it impossible to get along with. In this chapter we will explore what is happening and how to deal with this issue in a way that will allow you to become a more effective leader of a wide range of different people.

Part 3 - Five Key Behavioural Traits of Real Leaders in the Real World

In Part 3 we explore what we believe, and what our study suggests are the Five Key Traits that all Real Leaders in the Real World have.

Real Leaders in the Real World:

- Use Feedback to Succeed
- Take Considered Risks
- Are Forward Focused and Flexible
- Do what they Say and Say what they Do
- Develop Real Relationships with People

We will take you through each of these traits, explain what they are and why they are needed. We will help you to work out where your natural preferences are and show you how you can develop them in a way that fits with your personality and character.

To support your own growth as a leader we will identify where emotional regulation might be required to help you and how you can stretch your development to get better results, build great relationships and reach the top in your chosen area of leadership.

How to use this book

Our goal in this book is not only to provide some interesting information and knowledge around leadership. We want you to be able to do something practical and immediate with what you learn. We want you to become a leader in your own right, develop your existing leadership role and have an even greater positive impact in your life and that of those you lead.

The book is therefore split into clearly identifiable and separate chapters that can be taken individually to allow you to build up your own learning and practise each of the areas step-by-step.

The book has been structured in the order we believe will be easiest and most effective for you to learn. We suggest you read the whole book through first and then go back and use the particular chapter that is most relevant either to the issues you are facing at the time or the particular area of development you want to focus on.

You will become familiar with the structure of the book as you move through the chapters. In each one, we will talk about why it is important for leaders to develop this trait in themselves, what the different aspects you need to be thinking about are and how they are displayed, and how to identify your range of abilities and scope in the area.

We will then support you to decide how you want to develop each area and give you some ways and means to achieve this. This will involve some self-reflection and bringing ideas into your awareness, some activities you can do to develop yourself and some actions you can take to continue this development or even teach to others to help them develop too.

This world needs YOU!

We need more, better-developed and more capable leaders on this planet making a difference and we want you to be one of them.

By the time you have read this book we want you to be inspired to become a leader in your own world, know how to do it and know where to go from here. You will have learned the key attributes of what great leaders do, what your own style of leadership is, the strengths and limitations of it and you will know how to develop your style to maximise your impact as a leader.

By the time you have read this book (perhaps more than once) you will be able to take the risks that are needed, respond appropriately to what's happening around you, use feedback from the world in a way that helps you to move forward and develop healthy and mutually rewarding relationships. By being the real you, you will become a more fulfilled, purposeful and content human being and a Real Leader in the Real World.

CHAPTER 2

Emotional Regulation

"When dealing with people, remember you are not dealing with creatures of logic, but creatures of emotion."

Dale Carnegie

Before we get into the Real Problems of Real Leaders in Part 2 and the Five Key Behavioural Traits in Part 3, you need to understand more about emotional regulation. Why is it important? What is it? And what's its link to being a leader in the real world?

You may be tempted to move on to the later chapters, keen to get on and do something, get into some practical steps and not get into all that emotional stuff.

We would ask you to be patient. No tree-hugging or tissues required. The concepts and ideas in this chapter are essential to your understanding of what makes a good leader. It is equally, and arguably, more importantly the key to you having a less stressful, more fulfilling life. Quite a claim, we realise.

Emotional regulation is, we believe, the essential ability all leaders require to be inspirational, consistently effective and healthy leaders. We will talk about this concept and how it plays out in specific situations in further chapters of the book which will help you to get an appreciation of just how essential emotional regulation is and how, by developing your own, you will significantly increase your influence as a leader.

We said in Chapter 1 that we believe many of our leaders are not emotionally regulated. So what do we mean?

Let's start by looking at a definition of emotional regulation.

'Emotional regulation is the degree to which the emotions you are expressing in any given situation are appropriate to what is going on in that situation.'

It is an interesting term; we liken it to there being a thermostat in our body and brain which we can adjust to regulate our reaction to things happening around us. That's what it is really. Our nervous system sends chemicals around our bodies and brains to prepare us for the appropriate measured reaction to any given situation.

When our nervous system is emotionally regulated, the chemicals that are released are appropriate to the situation. When that happens, our behaviour is then appropriate to the situation and is likely to get an appropriate response from others. The problem for many of us is that our emotions are not as regulated as we think. Our emotions should be useful information, inside us, to guide us to appropriate decisions, actions and reactions. Think of the term emotion, there is the word motion in emotion, it is designed to move us. If we are emotionally unregulated, either our emotions are too strong for us to be able to make sense of them or are numbed, out of our conscious awareness. Either way is unhelpful.

Fight, Flight and Freeze

Most of you have heard of and understand the terms fight, flight or freeze as our instinctive responses to danger. This is hard-wired into each and every one of us at birth and is an essential safety mechanism in our body. It's really useful, until it's not.

The great thing about our fight, flight or freeze mechanism is that it fires automatically in response to a threat. The problem is that it fires automatically in response to a threat – whether that threat is real or not, it doesn't differentiate.

So why are we talking about this in a leadership book?

Well, because it is essential to be aware of this in yourself and others if you want to be a Real Leader. To be a Real Leader, to be clear thinking and have access to all the brilliant skills you have and to be able to take the risks you need to take, you need to be emotionally regulated.

We've been in many meetings, we're sure you have too, where someone flies off the handle at a seemingly trivial thing. There are many people who fear presenting more than death. A lot of people are scared to confront people about something they don't like. Have you ever reacted disproportionately to something? Have you been too heavy-handed, too emotional, too aggressive, too over the top, too shy? Have you ever seen the red mist?

Myth Buster - Shouting is Motivational

Shouting at other people, challenging them or putting people on edge (all tactics I have heard supposed leaders talk of using) is completely counterproductive and shows poor leadership skill, not to mention a lack of emotional regulation. Such behaviour is only likely to set off another person's fight, flight or freeze chemicals, depending on their preference, and will not produce any positive results.

These are all examples of when our emotional regulation is not working properly. We often don't realise this until after the event, because in the moment our emotions are hot-wired for survival and they just take over our body and behaviour. They are saying:

You must fight
You must run
You must freeze

directly into our spinal cord, flooding our body with chemicals.

This all happens in a millisecond, as it is meant to, and then afterwards we can often find ourselves trying to justify a behaviour that just happened!

When these fight, flight or freeze reactions happen it is because we have incorrectly coded something in our minds as dangerous, when it is not. This happened when we were very small with no cognitive reasoning ability and is often based on our own life experiences and beliefs. Most of us are unaware why they happen or that we can change them. The good news is we can. The first step is awareness.

Karen's example

"I remember once sitting in my car waiting for someone at the station, when a lady came over and knocked on the window and launched into a tirade about turning off my engine and how I was single-handedly destroying the planet. When she left I looked down at myself, I was shaking. This woman, although probably not very emotionally regulated herself, did not physically threaten me in any way and yet somehow my nervous system was thinking 'danger'. I was overreacting to the situation emotionally but I didn't realise it when the event was happening, I noticed it afterwards. That's how it happens; it's outside of our conscious awareness because it was coded in when we were very young."

We often have clients come to see us and the first thing they say is "I don't understand why I'm like this, I had a good childhood." It is an often thought misconception that in order to be emotionally unregulated, you need to have had a traumatic or difficult childhood. This is not so, we know a lot more now about the development of the brain than our parents did and certainly than their parents did. Small children have very strong emotions running around, all of the time – think of tantrums over biscuits and toys. Kids experience these emotions as pain, especially when they are very young, so how our emotions were dealt with as kids will define how we deal with those emotions when they surface as adults. Here are some of the things that have probably happened to most of us that will impact our emotional development:

- Our parents are tired and stressed when they hold us as babies – we pick up their emotional instability and code it as 'something's wrong' and feel scared.

- We had an illness as a child that meant a hospital stay without our parent there – we code this as being 'abandoned' and feel sad.

- Some other kid takes away the toy we are playing with – we code this as 'it's not fair' and feel angry.

- We are forced to sit at the table and eat all our food even though we are not hungry – we code this as embarrassing and feel shame.

If this happens even just a few times for us, it becomes coded into our mind and we react in a similar way, emotionally, for the rest of our life – until we become aware of it and do something different.

Our brains are not fully connected up until we are around five years old; before then we have no rational thinking so events get coded without our brain being fully wired up. This affects how we respond emotionally to everything thereafter, unless we do some personal development on emotional regulation to alter the neural pathways.

You can see how easily this happens. That's why a lot of behaviour we see doesn't make logical sense, but it does make perfect psychological sense.

Emotional regulation is naturally rare; we've not met anyone yet who is well-regulated without some form of personal development. Can we be completely emotionally regulated and have absolutely appropriate responses to everything in life? We don't know, we're still working on it, but the more emotionally regulated we can become, the easier it is for us to think clearly, maintain relationships, plan and solve problems.

Do you begin to see that to be a good leader you need to be able to develop your emotional regulation? Without it you will have problems thinking clearly, you are likely to be inconsistent in your behaviour, find yourself apologising or, worse, justifying a disproportionate response to something. If you are anything like us, you will have seen many a leader do this, some more regularly than others. Our question would be: What did you think of them when they did it?

Why do we do it?

We are back to those essential and sometimes less than helpful flight, flight or freeze chemicals running around our nervous system when there is not a clear and present danger threat. These chemicals block our brain's ability to have other more helpful chemicals available for other activities to allow us to respond appropriately or even think straight. Our fight, flight or freeze chemicals are on fast-track to our spinal cord, so take over our body (for the obvious survival reasons). If your life is being threatened there's not much requirement for being considerate for someone else's feelings because you might be dead in two minutes! When we are not emotionally regulated we literally can't think straight and as a result are unlikely to be at our best.

A lot of this is outside of our conscious awareness. It's like the hum of a computer going on in the background: we think it's normal until it turns off. It wasn't until Karen regulated her fear emotions that she realised how nervous she was most of the time (and yes, she's one of those people with that 'normal' upbringing). If it's outside of our awareness, how can we do anything about it?

Awareness is essential

The first step is to get some awareness, make it your mission to spot when you are reacting disproportionately to something.

You can get awareness of it by reflecting on your own thinking around situations and your behaviour in those situations. Was the behaviour appropriate, did you feel embarrassed by your behaviour or find yourself justifying the behaviour? In this book we will help you to identify what emotional regulation you might like to develop further and what you can do to do that. Don't worry, it's not that painful and no navel-gazing is required. Our brain has enough plasticity to develop new neural pathways until way into our 70s and 80s. We humans are magic like that.

Over the course of a few weeks, track your emotional regulation.

Notice situations where you become more angry or annoyed than the event really requires. Some typical situations might be:

- Getting annoyed or shouting at other drivers on the road. Unless someone actually crashes into you, when it would be appropriate for your survival chemicals to activate, this is disproportionate – really it is.

- Somebody arrives late to a meeting and you feel your frustration rise. Even when they apologise you can't seem to let it go emotionally.

- Your children don't like the dinner you've lovingly prepared for them. You stomp around the kitchen or shout at your partner.

- You're waiting to be served in a restaurant or café and the waiting staff seem to be ignoring you. You feel outraged.

Situations where you become more upset than the event really requires. Some typical situations might be:

- Someone is late and immediately you are worried they've had a serious accident or some other terrible disaster.

- You find yourself worrying a lot about things you have no control over.

- Your boss (or anyone else) criticises you and you feel tearful or cry. You feel hurt by their words.

- You watch something sad on TV and can't seem to shift the sad feeling once the programme is over.

- You get really upset when things go wrong for other people, sometimes even more than they seem to be.

Situations where you become more afraid than the event really requires. Some typical situations might be:

- You find it hard to sleep or relax – at all. These are usually indications of overactive fear chemicals.

- You are afraid to go and talk to someone at work about something that might end up being a difficult conversation.

- Any kind of procrastination or avoiding type behaviour. This is usually freeze chemicals kicking in.

- You are unhappy in your relationship and keep putting off having a conversation about it.

- You are not happy with the way your parents or in-laws talk to your children and you decide not to talk to them about it because you don't want to upset the applecart.

Situations where you feel more guilty or ashamed than the event really requires. Some typical situations might be:

- You feel bad because you haven't eaten all your dinner that someone else prepared. Or you eat all your dinner so as not to upset someone else, even when you are full.

- You take some time out for yourself and find yourself feeling bad or thinking about all the things you should be doing instead.

- If you use the word 'should' a lot. This word is particularly strong in people who have excessive guilt or shame feelings.

- You do something you want to do and then do lots of things for other people to 'balance things out'.

Situations where you feel numb or less than the event really requires. Some typical situations might be:

- You get some really good news, you know you should feel joy but you don't feel anything.

- Someone close to you dies and you can't feel grief.

- You have a car accident or some kind of safety 'near miss' but you don't experience any kind of adrenalin response.

- You feel as if you go through life not experiencing anything, just witnessing it like an observer.

If you find yourself disagreeing with us about the situations we describe here and believe that those reactions are proportionate, that is normal. You have run these patterns of behaviour all your life and have found lots of different ways to justify and explain yourself. So be easy on yourself and just start by noticing which emotion seems to stand out as disproportionate.

After awareness

There are many things you can do for yourself to help build your emotional regulation. Our suggestion is to work with a few of them at a time to maximise your success. As with everything in this book, the key to success is in building these into your natural habits and behaviours and become disciplined with them. If you only do them sporadically they will not be as impactful. We know you are busy and this may feel like a lot of work to begin with, but with practice they will become a natural part of your routine, like making your dinner or taking a shower.

Give your emotions a name

We don't mean call them Sally or Richard. Begin to give your emotions a label without attributing a cause. So by saying 'I feel angry' or 'I feel sad' it begins to regulate how your brain and body stores and recognises that emotion. Emotions are inside you not outside you. You've probably heard the phrase 'No one can make you feel anything' – it's true.

If we apportion our emotion outside of us, we give away our responsibility for our emotions to something outside us. The more you label or recognise your feelings and emotions without attributing them to an outside cause, the more your brain will begin to regulate and appropriately apportion your emotional responses. It often helps to agree with partners or work colleagues what you are doing, because some people will feel the need to act on your expression. Let them know that if you want them to do something about it you will ask them. Then the boundaries are clear and you can support each other.

Check in with yourself in the moment

Once you have awareness you can check in with yourself in the moment the emotional response is happening and say to yourself 'Is this is really appropriate to what's happening here?' If not, stop, take a deep breath and decide to react differently. Sometimes that means saying 'I'm not in the right place to deal with this right now, I'll come back to you'. Once you give yourself this information your brain will begin to recode it.

Controlled breathing

Your breathing is a hot-wire to your emotions; when our emotions are triggered our breathing changes. You can use these breathing exercises to release your repressed emotion. There is no need to wait until your emotions are triggered, you can practise this at any time. This works very well for fear and anger.

If you become more afraid than the event requires then practise breathing in for a count of 11 and breathing out for a count of seven. Do this slowly and breathe directly into your belly. Repeat this four or five times each time you practise it.

If you found you become more angry than the event requires then practise breathing in for a count of seven and out for a count of 11. Do this slowly and breathe directly into your belly. Repeat this four or five times each time you practise it.

Meditation

In the pile of 'easier said than done' we know, but so worth it. Studies of participants in meditation and forms of mindfulness have recently shown that the brain structure actually changes if you practise it regularly. More areas of your brain begin to activate which gives you access to more emotional clarity.

The problem with meditation is that it's not easy to keep your mind clear, our heads are often busy and it takes many weeks of practice before you begin to experience the benefits. It is worth it though, and even if you can do five minutes a day to start with, after four or five weeks you will notice a difference in how you feel and a positive difference in how you respond to events.

Here are some steps to meditation to get you started:

1. **Find a quiet spot**: It really doesn't matter where, as long as you can sit without being interrupted for a few minutes.

2. **Sit comfortably**

3. **Focus on your breath:** As you breathe in, follow your breath in through your nostrils, then into your throat, then into your lungs and belly. You can either do this with your eyes open and focused on a spot or have your eyes closed. As you breathe out, follow your breath back out. Sometimes it helps to count your breath in and out for four. If you find your mind wandering

(and you will), just pay attention to your mind wandering, then bring it gently back to your breath.

Do this for even just a couple of minutes each day and build it into a regular discipline for you.

Your physical wellbeing

We will talk a lot in this book about the psychological approaches to emotional regulation and they are very important to your success as a Real Leader. We also want you to pay attention to the physical aspects which can support your emotional regulation. In particular, focus on maintaining your blood sugar levels and, dare we say it, exercising!

What you put into your body has a significant contribution towards your emotional wellbeing. You can all relate to this, we're sure. If you've had a heavy night, a few glasses of wine and a curry you will generally feel more sluggish and fed up the next day than if you've eaten a healthy dinner and only allowed pure mountain spring water to pass your lips. When your body processes food and drink, it sends chemicals through your bloodstream and this impacts the chemical levels in your brain. Makes sense when you think about it. That's why you get moody or snappy when you are hungry, as Karen's friends will testify. If you're out for the day with Karen, regular snack breaks are essential or a meltdown may occur – it's not a pretty sight!

Our bodies are all different so there's no one eating programme which will suit everyone, nor would we suggest one. The key is to learn how your body works so that you can make sure you replenish what you need when you need it. There are some recommendations for books which you can use to help you with this at the end of the book.

As a general principle though, if you feel low, depressed or snappy, irritable or anxious, check in with yourself. Do you need something to eat or drink? It's amazing how you can make a feeling mean you're having a bad day or that something's going wrong when all you need is a banana and a glass of water. Really? Yes, really. Those of you who have kids will know this only too well – it's true for adults as well. In general, people do not drink enough water. Try consciously increasing your water intake each day and notice the changes in your energy levels and moods. Keep adjusting until you feel clear headed, resourceful and with good energy most of the time. When you are clear-headed, resourceful and energetic most of the time, this is a sign that you are maintaining appropriate levels of blood sugar in your body.

You'll be amazed how much this will impact your ability, effectiveness and success.

Spend time with people who you feel good with

Another way of emotionally regulating your brain is to

spend as much of your time as possible with people you feel relaxed with and see as your equal. Our brain structure and chemicals adjust depending on who we're with. If you are feeling uncomfortable, under threat in some way, your brain will adjust, ready for defence or attack as required. These brain chemicals are only really needed if there is a bus heading towards you or a lion is standing in front of you, licking his lips. They are not needed in the boardroom or the weekly sales meeting, yet we suspect, like us, you have often seen it there.

Relationships are wonderful. Simply having good relationships will automatically change your emotional regulation for the better just by being around these people. You know the type? When you are around them you feel good, relaxed, like a valuable member of the human race. They give you energy, they don't drain it away from you. They have no edge or agenda for you. After they leave, you feel like a better person just for having been around them. The Beatles' record producer used to say this of the Fab Four. Such people are the gold dust of emotional regulation. It's why some people transform when they meet the right partner in life or why children gravitate towards certain members of the family who are well-adjusted. Kids are chemical magnets, they will seek out the safest person in the room to go to for emotional regulation. If you've ever seen a child run up to you, sit on your lap or grab your hand for a few seconds then run off again, that's them coming for a bit of an emotional recharge. It's magic to watch.

Get these people into your life now!

Coaching and therapy

There's a bit of a stigma still in the UK about people seeing a therapist. It's almost like we need to be unable to function in the world and crying 85% of the time before we'd even look up a counsellor or a therapist. This is a shame as having a good therapist is like a superfast highway to emotional regulation. Coaching is very popular, it's the second largest part of our business, and is very useful and practical. The issue we have found is that many coaches have not had the psychological training or personal development of their own emotional regulation to support others with theirs.

If you are looking for some one-to-one support with your emotional regulation, the most important thing of all, regardless of their job title, qualifications and experience, is that the person is well emotionally regulated themselves. We're sad to say that even people who've had years of experience as a psychotherapist are not necessarily well emotionally regulated. The reason they need to be well emotionally regulated themselves is for the reasons we talked about in the previous section: your own brain structure will adjust according to who you are with and will start to rewire your own emotions. If the person who is supporting you professionally is not well emotionally regulated, your brain will know it and go on alert mode.

Ways to tell if your coach, counsellor or psychotherapist is emotionally regulated:

- You will feel safe and comfortable in their company. It's natural to feel a little nervous when you first meet someone, but you won't feel either under threat or overly sold to.

- You may find yourself getting emotional or saying things you hadn't planned to say. This indicates that your brain has picked up their emotional regulation and knows it's safe to express.

Watch outs – indications that your coach, counsellor or psychotherapist is not emotionally regulated:

- They spend most of the time in your session talking, usually about themselves.

- They are quick with advice and slow to understand.

- They make assumptions about you which you know are wrong.

- They ask you for reassurance or fish for compliments.

- They contradict themselves.

- You feel inferior to them (unless this is the issue you are working on, in which case you will feel like this with anyone).

- You feel manipulated in any way.

From our experience and the feedback of our clients, once the awareness comes and you are practising the suggestions above, it takes many of the negative feelings away. It allows you to stop blaming yourself or others and wasting energy unnecessarily.

In becoming the leader that you want to become you need to take responsibility for your behaviour. This does not mean control it and suppress it to the point that you become 'not human', there are enough people out there pretending to be that already. It means that you will express yourself appropriately in most situations (you are human so let's get real – you will not do it every time).

When you are expressing yourself appropriately you will begin to see people responding to you in a different way. When you are clear, they will hear you with clarity. When you are open, honest and direct they will respond to that and there will be less scope for confusion, argument or misunderstanding.

With emotional regulation you will have the control you need whilst also being real and that will make your message easier for people to understand and accept. When people feel that someone is in control, being straight with them and can be relied upon to behave in a consistent manner, they will relax, their own fear chemicals will not be fired and they will, themselves, be able to tap into their own skills and resources to support your goals and vision as their leader.

This is the simple truth. People respond to people, what they do, not just what they say. The more emotionally regulated you can become, the easier it is for people to feel they are safe with you. They will speak more openly and honestly with you because you are doing the same and they will see that you are in charge of yourself and therefore in charge.

Great leaders need emotional regulation. There's not as much out there as is needed. Start practising now.

PART 2

REAL
LEADERS,
REAL
PROBLEMS

CHAPTER 3

The Age Old Problem of Time

"The challenge of work/life balance is without question one of the most significant struggles faced by modern man."

Stephen Covey

There are so many people out there talking about the Holy Grail of a work/life balance. You need to do this or that, plan time with your family, leave the office on time at least twice a week, take time to stand on your head once a week (we made that one up but you get the idea).

The thing is, the phrase work/life balance doesn't make sense. It suggests that you have to balance your work with your life. Your work is part of your life so it's impossible to balance one against the other.

And anyway, what's wrong with working 15-hour days if you love what you do and it enriches and rewards you? There are many examples of people doing what they love and not seeing it as work. People like David Beckham and Richard Branson spring to mind as well as a number of our clients and students.

Working too much (We have yet to hear of anyone who has a work/life balance issue where the problem is they are doing too much life!) is only a problem if it affects your health or stops you doing something else that is more important to you. If neither of these is true, what's the problem?

From our Leadership Study

Quotes in response to the question:

"What are the main challenges you face in life at the moment?"

Lack of time to develop myself and read all the books I have bought
Never enough time
Spending a lot of time on things that benefit other people
Finding I have too little time to spend doing things I really enjoy myself
Oh man!!! Organisation of my life in general
Freeing up time to do what I want to do

There is so much talk about work/life balance because it is a problem for so many people. The problem that most people focus on is either they don't have the time they want to do all they want or they are doing things they have to do and then not having the time for what they want to do. This, we would suggest, is not the problem. The problem is your relationship with time, the beliefs and values you have around your time and the choices you make around how you spend your time. Notice what we are saying here: how you spend your time – not how you use it, what you need to do in it, but how you spend it.

Myth Buster - Time

Everyone in the world has the same amount of time in each day: 24 hours. How you spend it is your **choice**.

Whilst some of the leaders in our study highlighted the work/life balance as an issue – 25% of them – the vast majority, 75%, felt that the balance worked well most of the time. Admittedly we didn't ask their life partners if they agreed with the assessment!

Yet it is interesting that three-quarters of those surveyed felt it worked well. What is it they are doing that others do not? Let's be clear here: many of them cited too much work and too little time as challenges, so it's not that they have less work or feel that they deal with the work better – so how can that be true? The key is that overall they felt their life and work flowed well.

Anyone who has been on a time management course will tell you that they have varying degrees of success because of one simple fact: how we use our time has much more to do with our psychology than our ability to be organised. There are two key factors in play when it comes to how we 'do' time: how we code time in our minds and what's important to us, our values.

How do you code time?

We all code time differently in our minds; we have a client who sorts her time into 15-minute slots and some clients who sort their time in months. Both ways have their benefits and drawbacks. Our 15-minute client is mega-efficient and packs a lot into her day but also finds it hard to relax and gets anxious about time. Our clients who sort by months are very relaxed and enjoy going with the flow – this makes them great fun to be around. The drawback comes when they turn up in the wrong office on the wrong day for an important meeting. They are not forgetful, they know what's happening this month, just not specifically this day.

How do you code and sort your time? Minutes, half days, weeks, months, years?

One indicator of this is what kind of diary style do you like? Month view, week view or day, hour-by-hour view?

This is really useful to know, because you can organise your life to suit your preference for sorting time and you are aware of the problems you might experience with this and know what to do to help yourself.

Generally speaking, the smaller your time chunks, the more detailed you need to be in your organisation and planning. If you were organising a party, someone with small time chunks needs to have specific actions and to-do's that help them. Having an action like 'plan party' will just send you into overwhelm or paralysis, so breaking things down into smaller bits will help. For example, drawing up a guest list or researching venues.

Someone with larger time chunks would find this approach stifling and restrictive. If this is you, think in terms of what you want to achieve this month or week rather than specific tasks. Taking the 'plan party' example again, someone with larger time chunks should have an outcome like 'by the end of this month, I will have selected a venue'. They don't need to know when they will specifically do the internet research, speak to the venues and then visit. It will happen in the flow of life for them.

If you are finding your current way of sorting time is not working for you, this may be because you have picked it up from someone else. But here's the thing: just because it works for them doesn't mean it will work for you. That's why many of these time management courses, whilst interesting, are useless. Experiment with planning in different time chunks until you find a way that works best for you.

How your time sorting creates stress

All ways of sorting time have their issues and these are worth being aware of – how you could stress yourself out and what you can do about that.

Small chunks

People who sort time into smaller chunks – minutes or hours – will inevitably try to pack too much into each day and may have issues with exhaustion and tiredness. Because they feel good when they get things done, they may end up doing a lot of activity without thinking about why they are doing it or how it fits into the big picture of their lives. They might also have trouble linking their activity to the purpose of life and therefore feel unfulfilled and empty sometimes.

If this is you, take time every now and then (within an hour slot of course!) to think consciously about how your activity benefits your life as a whole. Are there things which have become just habits, you've become fixated on (like Karen's mum's need to hoover every day – only two of them live in the house!)? By doing this you begin linking your activity back to your life and this will help you to sort out what's working and what's not. With practice and regular review of what you do, you will begin to sense what adds to your life and what does not, thereby freeing up some spare time to do other things. Spare time. If this phrase makes you laugh or tut out loud or brings you out in a cold sweat then you need to work on this right away.

Middle chunks

People who sort in mid-time chunks – days or weeks – can get overwhelmed or stressed when they have a full day or week. They can also get lost in activity, sometimes not linking it to the benefit of their life overall.

Karen is a good example of someone who works in mid-chunks.

She looks at a busy day with lots of appointments or a busy week with lots of training and goes "Oh my (or similar phrase!), there's no room in here for unexpected interruptions." Knowing that this can stress her out, and causes John pain, Karen makes sure she blocks out a few hours here and there in the week when she can attend to these things should they crop up. Karen also takes time to link in her activity to what it means for her. For example, has she seen all the friends that are important to her in the space of a few months? You can't fit everyone and everything into a week so expanding your time chunks will really help.

Big chunks

People who sort in larger time chunks may have problems with prioritising and deadlines. "No 'may' about it", says John.

They are likely to underestimate how long things take to do. We have a friend who says everything takes ten minutes – he finds it hard to get anything done.

People who sort time in larger chunks can end up feeling despondent and irritated because they don't get as much done as they had hoped or expected. If you are someone who sorts time this way, what will really benefit you is having a good (small time chunk sort) second-in-command or PA to keep you on track and make sure you don't forget things.

A lot of entrepreneurs we know fit into this category and the benefit of a 'different time sort' second-in-command or PA is of great value. It allows the entrepreneur to focus on what they are good at and for the other important things to be done by the other person who is much more capable at it. Whilst we can all stretch ourselves and learn to do that which we are not as comfortable with, we will never be as good as the person who does it naturally. A lot of time and money can be saved when you realise this and allow people to play to their strengths.

Another way is to set aside time for doing things that don't excite you but need doing. John has what he calls his 'Admin Dog Days' where he does all his diary organising and admin. The rest of the team are not allowed to call him or interrupt him at these times because he will happily get distracted on to something else. The key is not to set aside too much time for this if you sort time in big chunks; half a day is usually as much time as you can stand without drifting off into something else.

Practise with what works best for you until you can get into as much flow as works for you. Here's the thing though: time will always be one of those unresolvable dilemmas. We only have 24 hours in a day, 365 days in a year, so many years in our life, so no one will have this perfectly sorted. It's something to refine and manage constantly and when you learn to have a more relaxed relationship with time, life becomes a lot easier.

As a leader, if you can work with your own time preference and that of the team around you, then you can create a well-blended team that has all the skills required to deliver what is needed to succeed and become the best.

What's important to us

Once you've worked out how to sort your time in a way that works for you, the next thing is to decide what to do in those time chunks. This is where our psychology comes in again – what's important to us, our values.

Myth Buster - Values

Our values are things we are willing to spend time, money and resources either to achieve or to avoid. They are often outside our conscious awareness. If you want to ascertain someone's values, observe what they do with their time; that – not what they say – is important. What they say is likely to be aspirational, not what's really driving them.

There is an enormous amount of complexity in the topic of values and much of it is beyond the scope of this book. The key aspect of values we want to talk about here relates to how they affect your ability to manage your time more effectively.

We will only do activity that's important to us at some level, even if what we are doing is not making us happy or is actually creating stress for us. When it comes to the age old problem of time, it is your values that drive your habitual behaviour. Where you have an issue with time, as some of our leaders in the study had, what you need to do is regularly review how you are spending your time.

Most of what we do is habitual, which makes our life a little easier and more predictable, and even if you believe you have a career or lifestyle that is constantly changing, there will always be a pattern to it. When you understand that pattern, it will help you to recognise how you deal with time and change it for the better.

Identifying your behaviours relating to time

One technique we use with the leaders we work with that they find useful is to have them regularly review how they actually spend their time to identify where it works well and where it doesn't. When it flows and when they get stuck, overworked or stressed.

A version of this technique you can do for yourself is this:

Take time at the end of the week to review the activity of the week. Ask yourself:

- What did I achieve this week?

- What didn't I achieve that I wanted to? Why didn't I achieve it? (avoid blaming other people or things)

- How do I feel I used my time?
- When was I in control of my time and when was I not? When I wasn't, who was?

Here is another useful technique you can use in the moment:

Ask yourself when you're in the middle of an activity 'Why am I doing this?' and notice what pops into your mind. If you do this enough you will get a sense of what's really driving your behaviour.

Once you get conscious awareness of what's driving your behaviour you can decide whether you want to change it or not.

Are there other, more beneficial ways to spend your time to achieve the same purpose for you?

Choose only a few things to work on at a time and refine and adjust them as you need to.

There is no need to lead busy fools; get smart about time

As a leader, identify what is important to you and as far as you can, do that. Utilise the resources of other people who have the skills and enjoy the things you don't. It will make you and your organisation, family or charity much more effective and efficient. You do not need to be able to do everything. You can lead by example without actually having to do it all.

When you can understand how you use your time and how to manage your time better, it will allow you to maintain your emotional regulation much more easily. It will create an air of calm and control both inside you and as a projection out to other people. When you are calm it radiates out to other people, which in turn helps them to be calm and therefore they will be more effective and efficient in their activity.

We have seen many situations, whether it be a business or a family, where there is a culture of 'too much to do and not enough time'. It becomes a mantra and almost a badge of honour that they both wear and complain about at the same time. We have worked with many leaders where they believed that this was just the way it was and could not be changed. This isn't the case.

Busy for busy's sake and too much work and not enough time shows a lack of leadership and is not a motivational tool! If everyone is too busy most of the time, you have a problem. Not one of too much work, but one of not enough leadership. Being too busy is a choice and you can choose to change it by taking the time to look at what is really going on, what is important to you and what you want to do about it.

This takes strong leadership and often involves swimming against the tide as there is a belief in many countries and cultures that we have to be busy, there is always too much to do and we just have to keep going and do what we can or work ourselves to a standstill, which is simply not the case.

It is a simple self-fulfilling prophecy. The more you are under stress, the more work you have to do or time pressure you are under, the less emotionally regulated you are, the less resourceful you are and the less effective you are. This results in you achieving less in more time, adding to your time issues and stress and so the loop goes around.

Stop, analyse what is going on, prioritise and emotionally regulate your behaviour and you will do more in less time or do better in the same time or – and wait for it – do what's needed in less time and have more time for expansive thinking, strategy or, dare we say it, time off and relaxation. If you are shouting 'impossible' or 'delusional' at this point, you are being controlled by others and need to take charge of your own time. Lead by example.

CHAPTER 4

The Age Old Problem of Other People

"If you want plenty of experience in dealing with difficult people, then have kids."

Bo Bennett

Other people. Can't live with them, can't live without them. It's one of the unresolvable dilemmas of leadership, not to mention life.

John is always telling Karen that if only she thought and behaved in exactly the same way as he does then everything would flow smoothly, there would be no issues in life and the world would be an easier, calmer and generally better place. Karen's response to this is not fit for public consumption.

From our Leadership Study

Quotes in response to the question:

"What aspects of your leadership position do you dislike?"

Others' slowness to get the idea
Fixed mindsets and unwillingness to change
Politics just bores me
Command and control management styles in others
Dealing with control freaks and ego driven people
People who are switched off and need to be carried
Performance managing people
People who only think in boxes
Having to deal with negative people

The point is we all know that everyone is different – how many of you say it and believe it? "Yes everyone is different and it's so wonderful to have difference in the world and it makes it a wonderful kaleidoscope, an adventure, blah blah blah..."

This difference is all well and good but when you are trying to do something brilliant and you are surrounded by 'other people' it doesn't feel so wonderful. You know you are right, it's just everyone else. Why don't they listen and just do what you ask? How hard can it be?

Sound familiar? It does to us and to most of the leaders involved in our study.

From our Leadership Study

Quotes in response to the question:

"Which qualities do you dislike in other people?"

The nay sayers
Wishy washy behaviour
Blaming others for their response to the situation
Back-stabbing
Over inflated self-importance
Bullies
Micro managers
Jobsworth people – 'the computer says no'
Not paying enough attention to the detail
Over concern with the small stuff
Arrogance

90% of our research participants said that working with and developing other people is a part of the role they enjoyed and yet 63% of participants in our research highlighted some kind of difficulties with other people as something they disliked about their position.

As a leader, the problem is that you are no one if there is no one to lead. Just because you are head of a company doesn't make you a leader, it just makes you a business owner. This is why relationships and problems with other people are a key concern and focus for all good leaders. And so it should be. There was no particular pattern of the types of behaviours that participants in our study highlighted in terms of the context of leadership. It seems that regardless of whether you are a leader in business, a community group or a charity, the same types of behaviours in others were problematic.

Getting Real on People Problems

We are not going to promise you that we can solve all your difficult people issues. Let's be real, you can't like everyone. In our experience working with leaders over many years, the only people who've said they like everybody are either delusional or have very low self-esteem. If you are a leader you have an opinion, you stand out, you have a style that is all yours. That is going to clash with some people. That doesn't make you right or wrong, it makes you human. It's a sad fact that not everyone will like you, regardless of how amazing you think you are.

We will talk much more about developing real relationships later in the book; for now we want to focus on the problem behaviours, help you to understand them a bit more and decide what, if anything, you can do about them. Sometimes being a Real Leader is about accepting that people are where they are and you just have to leave it. But there are a few steps before that.

It's a matter of perspective

First of all, let's be clear: all interpretation of someone else's behaviour is a matter of perspective, your own. We dislike the behaviour because we have made a judgment about its meaning. Most likely we have not gone right up to these people and said "You seem to be very small-minded and have an overinflated view of your abilities, am I right?" And they say "Yes that's right." We don't have this conversation very often. We could be right in our assessment of the meaning, or not. It's worth considering what else the behaviour could mean.

Looking at the study results, there are also some contradictory statements. One person said 'Not paying enough attention to the detail' and another said 'Overly concerned with the small stuff'. It all depends on your own position whether you value some skills in other people or not. A 'wishy washy' person could be quite creative and get value in holding uncertainty for some time. This can be a great skill in some roles.

Common unlikeable behavioural traits

Let's look now at three of the most common unlikeable behavioural traits that came out of our research and our experience of the types of things we are asked to help our clients with more often than anything else.

We will talk you through what is usually going on psychologically for people who demonstrate each of these behaviours. Whilst not everyone will fit this pattern, most people will and we have provided some effective ways you can use that will help to deal with the behaviour and are likely to get the best outcome for everyone involved. Remember also that your perception of these behaviours may be something for you to work on as the problem with other people's behaviour might well be how you are seeing these behaviours. We will talk more about this here too.

Problem Behaviour - Laziness

How do you know someone is lazy? Really. What specific observable behaviours do you see?

One person's lazy is another person's reflector. If you are a fast-paced, action, action, action, KAPOW! sort of person, it is likely you will notice more lazy people. Because you are a one man (or woman) mission to save the world from any unfinished task, avoid any chance to reflect on ANYTHING, and generally keep moving at all costs, anyone who is not doing the same will appear slow, ploddy and lazy. This is an issue of your perception and something that it will help you to get awareness of.

Myth Buster - Leaving work on time

Leaving at 5pm, if that's the work finish time, is not sloping off early. It often shows good time management and efficient work practices and suggests high self-esteem in that person. Any negative reaction you have to that is your issue not theirs.

If this is not you and someone appears to be generally not capable of getting things done, they seem to procrastinate or slope off early, then before you take action we suggest you take some time to understand what may be going on for them.

Often people who exhibit the behaviours associated with laziness have too many freeze chemicals (remember flight, flight and freeze chemicals from Chapter 2?) running around in their brain. They are basically terrified at some level of getting things wrong, making a mistake or being told off. When stress kicks in they freeze, they put their head in the sand and hope that it will all go away. This kind of behaviour goes way back to childhood and is common in people who have excessive shame emotions.

'If I do nothing, I can get nothing wrong.'

This doesn't make logical sense, but it makes perfect psychological sense. Knowing this can help you to tackle the behavioural issues in a way that sets the best foundation possible for overcoming them.

What to do - ask if they need help

You probably want to kick them up the backside, and whilst we understand it is tempting, this action will only hit more of their fear chemicals and cause them to freeze more. If your outcome is to get to the heart of the issue and resolve it for the long term, start by asking them if they need help. Approach them in a supportive and non-patronising way. Go on an information gathering mission with them: What specifically do they find challenging? Who else could help? Do they need some training? Are they clear on what they are trying to do?

Sometimes people do not understand what you are asking them to do; this doesn't make them stupid, just different from you. For example, if you are a visionary thinker your instructions will make no sense to a detail-oriented person. You will appear fluffy and vague. Yet you need detail-oriented people to deliver your plan, and making sure they know what they are doing and are comfortable with it will save a lot of time, money and unnecessary frustration.

As a leader, taking a curious and supportive approach with people who seem to be lazy will help to calm down their freeze chemicals and give you both the best chance of working through the issue. Give it a go, what have you got to lose? And you may be surprised at how well it works.

Problem Behaviour - Arrogance

How do you know someone is arrogant? Really. What specific observable behaviours do you see?

One person's arrogant is another person's confident. If you are someone who has a low sense of confidence, it is likely you will notice more arrogant people. Because you are not confident in your own abilities, anyone who is will appear cocky and have an overinflated opinion of themselves. This is an issue of your perception and something that it will help you to get awareness of.

> ## Myth Buster - Arrogance does not reflect confidence
>
> When a person displays what most people will agree is arrogant behaviour, don't get annoyed or envious of their confidence. Feel sad for them. Arrogance is simply a smokescreen for very low self-esteem and the shame they feel.

If this is not you, and someone's behaviour seems to be creating a problem for other people, not just you, then you have someone on your hands with low self-esteem, who uses arrogance to try to mask it. The more over-the-top the behaviour, the lower their self-esteem is. This may sound ridiculous to you and it's true. People who are overly arrogant probably never got that much praise as a child so the only person who can tell them they do a good job is, well, them. This is often practised over time to the point it becomes a habit in the hope that one day they might actually believe they are good enough.

'If I keep telling other people how great I am, eventually I might believe it myself, one day.'

What to do - Give them positive feedback

The problem with arrogant behaviour is that the last thing you want to do with them is to give them any positive feedback, we get that. Whilst it can feel counterintuitive, if you are their leader and you want to help them, it can be a really constructive way of moving this person on. Your outcome is to help them to get an accurate sense of their performance, and if all you do is point out the things they don't do well, that only feeds the low self-esteem pain the person feels and your action will only make them more arrogant and defensive. This pain is all unconscious; they may be completely unaware of what is triggering the behaviour, all they know is what they've always known and they will protect themselves the only way they know how.

As a leader, begin to observe and give positive feedback on the things they do well. This has to be genuine or it will not be received as real. Don't do platitudes – people can spot them a mile off. Notice what they do well, specifically, and give them positive feedback on it.

Over time you can then begin to balance this with behaviours you want them to improve. They are more likely to hear it if they also feel they are being noticed for the good things they do. They will be less defensive and so the old behaviour is less likely to be triggered and they will respond in a more positive way. This will take some time of course, and it will take much less time and money than continually having to deal with the consequences of the arrogant and defensive behaviour.

We have given this advice to many organisations over the years and whilst they had the same initial reaction to this advice as you are probably having now, they did it and were amazed at the results.

Problem Behaviour - Bullies

How do you know someone is a bully? Really. What specific observable behaviours do you see?

One person's bully is another person's assertive. If you like people to be nice and shy away from conflict, it is likely you will notice more bullies. Because you are afraid of conflict, anyone who is assertive and OK with conflict will appear aggressive, forceful and disrespectful. This is an issue of your perception and something that it will help you to get awareness of.

Myth Buster - Bullying is never acceptable

We often hear people being told, in the face of what is bullying behaviour, that they need to toughen up. This is completely misguided and ineffective. At best you create two bullies, at worst someone gets bullied more or retreats into their shell.

If this is not you and someone's bullying behaviour is causing an issue to others as well as you, then you have someone who is very emotionally unregulated on your hands. People with bullying behaviour were probably bullied as a child – by their parents, siblings or at school. They saw that it got some positive results; they got their own way, and so the bully in them emerged. These people have a lot of repressed anger, so when it comes out it comes out as overly aggressive and disproportionate.

'Attack is the best form of defence, get in first, be loud and aggressive and people will do what you say, and then I don't have to feel bad.'

Unfortunately bullying behaviour has become the cultural norm in some businesses and this can make it quite difficult to deal with. When people accept that the loudest, most aggressive behaviour wins, then they are effectively saying that this behaviour is OK. It's not, ever. We see far too much of it in all aspects of life – in families as well as organisations. It affects people's self-esteem, confidence and ultimately their health and it is always counterproductive.

What to do - Address the behaviour

Bullies are effectively children. They need an adult to deal with them. Their behaviour comes from a feeling of weakness, not strength.

Example

We heard a story recently of a leader in an organisation saying to his line managers that they need to be more challenging and aggressive towards each other so the people below them would see how strongly they felt about things, how important it was and how committed they were to the business. As is often the case, this is simply bullying behaviour dressed up as 'being challenging' and does not work. The leader's intention was to generate energy, increase direct and clear communications between people and ultimately increase morale and commitment. The opposite happened. People became more frightened (fight, flight, freeze) spoke up less, hid more, covered their tracks more and morale fell and people began to leave.

The first thing you need to do if you want to deal with bullying behaviour is to make sure you are as emotionally regulated as you can be. Their behaviour is designed to hit your fear buttons so you've got to work on that first.

When you are emotionally regulated, begin to set boundaries as cultural norms within your organisation or family that will not allow bullying behaviour to flourish. You are the leader so you need to lead this. This doesn't mean attacking the bully back with equally aggressive behaviour. They need to get absolutely no positive payback from their bullying behaviour.

You need to make it clear in your own behaviour that bullying is not acceptable, and this doesn't just mean saying so. You have to deal with it.

Some ways which work well with bullying behaviour are:

- If someone is acting this way, tell them that you will speak to them about this when they are in a more appropriate state. You need to say this in a straightforward, factual way. Any hint of patronising or aggressive behaviour from you will just make them worse. If necessary, tell them to come back tomorrow at a certain time to discuss it. That way you are saying that you want to talk about this issue, you realise it's important and you are not going to do that while they are behaving like this.

- If they are standing, stand up as well to match their height and stature as far as possible. Ask them to tell you what the issue is, keep the language impersonal and the tone of voice measured, firm and clear. It will help take the heat out of a situation.

- If this behaviour is happening in a meeting or a public place, you have to be clear that it is not an acceptable way to behave. Find an appropriate time to interrupt or change the subject, invite other people's views. Avoid shaming the person if at all possible as that is what's made them like this in the first place. If you can have their dignity in mind when dealing with them, that will usually create the best outcome.

- Model the behaviour you want other people to do. If you stand up to a bully, so will other people. If you do nothing and then later go and make it up to the person who got attacked, you are just making things worse. If you show that you will not accept this behaviour, other people will soon follow you. The message will be heard quickly by the bully.

Of course, there are some situations when the problem is so bad these approaches will not work and then you need to deal with the person head on, removing them if necessary. This is more likely to happen if you let it go or put it off as the message you give to the bully and everyone else is that the behaviour is acceptable at some level. Letting it go will give you constant problems to deal with, destroy morale and ultimately make you look weak. It will not go away.

Becoming Difficult People-Proof

We're not suggesting these approaches will always work, but they will give you a chance of resolving the issue and will work in many situations. In the situations where it doesn't work completely, we guarantee that you will get some useful information about what's going on in the process. That information will then help you decide what course of action you want to take next.

With this new found knowledge, it might be tempting to say to someone "I understand you have self-esteem issues and that's why you are behaving this way." Please don't – it will not be received well! These issues are often held at an unconscious level for the person so they will not believe what you are saying and will react – they are unlikely to say thank you.

Wherever possible, think about how you can resolve the issue whilst keeping everyone's dignity intact. You might have to take more direct action at some point, but if you tackle the behaviour early and start with a low-level intervention, then you can gradually move up the level of intervention, if required, knowing that you've done all you can to resolve this in a way that sought to respect everyone. Often leaders leave these behaviours to fester to the point where they stand out so much, they are often at the point of no return. Start early and avoid big problems later.

In this chapter we have also given you a sense of where your unresolved issues might be. If you are reacting to someone's behaviour, what is this hitting in you?

Becoming difficult people-proof is also about working on your own areas of self-development so that behaviour doesn't affect you emotionally, it's just behaviour. This is why working on your own emotional regulation is so important.

The issue is not always directly obvious so give this some thought. If you find aggressive people hard to deal with, it's doesn't necessarily mean you are an angry or aggressive person (although you might be). It may be that you are unpractised at dealing with conflict situations; you may not have learned a productive way of doing this as a child. If so, start by dealing with issues early, practise with low-level conflicts until you feel more comfortable dealing with them.

The examples we have used in this section are the most common problems we hear about in our work with leaders and prospective leaders. The key messages from each of these can be applied to most 'difficult people' issues and we want you to become skilled and practiced in each of them. Given the time we all spend interacting with other people – whether at work, at home or socially (which is a lot unless you are a hermit) – these skills and ways of thinking are essential for a more fulfilling and less stressful life. It will not only help you in leadership, it will help you in life in general. The more emotionally regulated you are, the more curious you become about others' behaviour; and the less you are negatively impacted by them, the more energy and time you will have for whatever you like to do.

When it comes to the age old problem of other people, we want you to always be thinking 'How much of it is me?'

If not me, what is going on behind these behaviours and how can I deal with it in a more useful way?

Good leaders take the time and have the skill and patience to deal with the root problem of others' unhelpful behaviour and avoid constantly and repeatedly wasting time, energy and resources dealing with the symptoms.

PART 3

FIVE KEY
BEHAVIOURAL
TRAITS OF
REAL LEADERS

CHAPTER 5

Use Feedback to Succeed

"Feedback is the breakfast of champions."

Ken Blanchard

What do you have for breakfast?

Feedback is a funny thing. Lots of people do it, most of us have received it and yet, from our experience, it is not often well done or, when received, well used.

In this chapter we will explore what feedback is, the sources of feedback and help you to gain awareness of your inner feedback to yourself and how you take in feedback from other people.

A healthy relationship with feedback

To be a good leader, to be a success and to encourage and motivate others requires you to pay attention to and use feedback well.

All too often leaders pay either far too much or far too little attention to feedback. When you pay too much attention you think it shows that you are listening and responding to what is needed. In reality you can often appear weak and indecisive, changing your mind with every new bit of information. On the other hand, when you pay too little attention to feedback you think it shows strength, decisiveness and that you know what you are doing. In reality, you can often appear arrogant, out of touch and unapproachable.

As a leader, having a healthy relationship with feedback will avoid you losing touch with your team, failing to achieve your goals and missing the opportunity to be the best. When you have a healthy relationship with feedback, your team will respect and engage with you, you will use feedback to continually improve and will have the information you need to reach the top.

Do you know how you or your business is doing? How do you know? Where do you get your feedback from? Do you even care about it?

From our Leadership Study

Quotes in response to the question:

"What would you describe as your keys to success?"

Listen and seek to understand
Understand that other people have good ideas too
Ability to stand back and understand more than the presenting problem
Ability to quickly assess a problem and take action
Observation, making sense of what's going on

Using feedback to inform you and help you decide on actions and decisions is a key trait of good leaders. Classically though, the word feedback brings back shudders and hyperventilation caused by bad appraisal experiences and the sh*t sandwich – when people try to dress up something they want you to do by saying something nice to you first, then sliding in the criticism.

This is not what we mean by feedback.

What do we mean by Feedback?

Here is the Oxford dictionary definition of feedback:

1. Information about reactions to a product, a person's performance of a task, etc. which is used as a basis for improvement.

2. The modification or control of a process or system by its results or effects, for example in a biochemical pathway or behavioural response.

There are some key points to this definition which we are interested in:

1. It's to do with gathering information, from which you can make improvements.

2. You can modify what you are doing by assessing results and effects.

This is what we mean by feedback and good leaders do feedback well. Where you get your feedback from and what feedback you pay attention to can be your strength and your limitation as a leader.

Wisdom comes from multiple perspectives so if you only get feedback from the same source, you will be missing something. Depending on your psychological preferences you will also pay attention to certain types of feedback. By stretching yourself in both these areas, you will have a wealth of information to help you to make decisions, assess your success and inform the future.

Sources of Feedback

We all have our favourite sources of feedback and this is generally driven by what we, personally, consider to be the most important influence on our business, family or life. Some business leaders are most interested in the figures, the bottom line; some family leaders' main interest is in how they appear to the outside world. For some charity leaders all that matters is the impact of their work on the community. We know companies who use feedback from staff as a key driver for their strategy. Our personal favourite is feedback from delegates and clients.

Which is the best? All of them and more. If you only ever pay attention to your favourite forms of feedback you are missing a whole heap of information which could be helpful to you as a leader. Let's look at some of the possible sources of feedback available.

Statistics and Figures

If you don't love the numbers and you are in business, find a way of loving them. Leaders who glaze over at the sight of a spreadsheet find that turning the numbers into a story of the business helps them to be connected to this. If your financial director can't do this, find another financial director. Don't ever feel stupid about not understanding what the figures are telling you; use the expertise in your business, community project, charity, or even household to help you. If it doesn't exist there are loads of ways of getting help with this: your relationship manager at your bank, money websites and a number of companies run training courses to help leaders use figures to support them.

Your Staff

Staff are often a missed source of valuable information. The problem is they often assume that, as the leader, you know what they know, so wouldn't think to tell you. We see it all the time when working with senior management teams in business. Pieces of information come up and you see light bulbs go on around the table; no one thought to raise it before because they thought it was obvious.

Staff surveys are often deemed a waste of time on both sides because nothing ever happens or is reported back as a result of it. The key to successful staff surveys is to be clear on the outcome of the survey. Do you want feedback on products, operating processes, staff satisfaction? Never try to do them all at once. Be clear what you are going to do as the result of the survey. We often find it is more effective to do short surveys people can complete in five to ten minutes on very specific subjects rather than one yearly survey marathon.

Don't always just ask the obvious people. The marketing department may not be the best people to advise you on a new product or service. Rich sources of feedback can come from the most unusual sources. A company we worked for has regular feedback focus groups with the reception staff and security people because they touched so many parts of the business, could hear what people chatted about in reception, how visitors were received and treated and were a rich source of company gossip. Never underestimate anyone's ability to provide feedback.

Your Boss

You are probably used to your boss giving you feedback at formal occasions like appraisals and it's likely you'll know when you've done something they disapprove of. Do you use them as a rich source of feedback to help you to learn and develop from?

This doesn't mean asking them 'How did I do?' after every task, which will, quite frankly, drive them mad. What we mean is ask smart questions, and (going back to our definition of feedback) use the answers you get to help you make improvements or modify something.

Smart questions like:

What specifically did you think went well with that project/meeting?

Do you think we could have done any more on...?

I'm wondering, was I too 'X' in that meeting, what do you think?

Getting these little snippets of feedback can be really helpful, if you have the emotional regulation and confidence to ask.

Myth Buster - Feedback is not an order

Just because someone has said it doesn't mean you should do it. It's feedback for your information not action.

Your Peers

If you are the boss and have no one above you to ask, then peer feedback is going to be really important for you though potentially more difficult to get. When you are in that position, can you find a peer in a different part of the organisation, a friend who runs their own business, someone in your family you trust or find an experienced coach you can talk to?

At any level of leadership and in any context of leadership, whether it be business, family or community, peer feedback can be very valuable. We're not talking about a 360 degree feedback operation here, although you may use that process if it is relevant. Getting a clear sense of how others see you will help you get a true sense of whether your perception of yourself and what others perceive matches. The key thing about peer feedback is that you are looking for themes and patterns, not reacting to every piece of feedback you receive. People are all different, so they will notice different things. Here's our suggestion on how to assess peer feedback:

1. If you are getting feedback that conflicts, ignore it. Examples include someone saying you are too detailed and someone else saying you need to pay attention to detail. You cannot be both – this will be about them not you.

2. Look for themes in the feedback. Look above (and avoid reacting to) individual comments.

3. Decide what you would like to do as a result of what you have learned.

Your Clients

Your clients will be giving you feedback when they buy or don't buy something – true. But if this is all you use you are missing another rich source of information. Getting into the clients' shoes is about more than just finding out if they will buy something or not.

Have regular get-togethers with the people in your organisation who have direct contact with clients and ask 'What are people talking about? Asking questions about?' and really listen to the response.

When Karen ran a large call centre, her managers would spend a few hours each week taking calls from customers and then have a regular meeting to discuss the themes of feedback. The feedback was so valuable and informed new products, services and processes.

Some leaders take part in 'back to the floor' type exercises where they get direct access to customers in a natural way, and this can be very valuable too.

Focus groups can be helpful, but they are often very formal and have a preordained intention (e.g. would they buy this product or service?) so clients often feel a bit interrogated and the facilitators have a script so they might cut off clients in their flow. Karen had a situation in a former company she worked for when she and her other managers were behind a two-way mirror listening to a focus group talking about investments and one client began to talk about his view on investing in property. The facilitator stopped him because that wasn't the purpose of the group. Karen recalls: "We all sat there with our head in our hands, whatever he had to say would have been so useful to know and we never got to hear."

So the more you can interact with clients naturally, the better the feedback. If you run a restaurant, eat in there sometimes with your clients around you, you'll be amazed what you pick up. Retail leaders go and shop in their stores and learn so much about buying behaviour from this. In our trainings we have a formal process for clients to give us feedback and we are listening to them all the time, the feedback often comes to us indirectly.

The Competition

Some leaders are preoccupied with what the competition is doing. Some leaders ignore them. Neither of these approaches is right or wrong in itself, the key is how does what you are doing support and inform your actions and decisions? Does the information on your competitors confuse you and make you question your decisions or is it useful data in deciding future strategy? Are you missing valuable information about the marketplace by not paying attention to what the competition is doing?

Feedback from the competition can be about more than the thing you are in competition on. Many industries now have a much more collaborative attitude with their competition than in the 'dog-eat-dog world' of the past. Many leaders realise that competitive advantage is about much more than doing the same thing cheaper, better or faster.

Your competitors can give you feedback about the supporting systems and services they use which could support a decision you may be making. A client of ours was looking at a new operating system and found out that a key competitor was doing the same. They decided to approach the tendering process together and although they made different decisions about who to go with, they learned valuable things from each other about the potential benefits and drawbacks of each alternative.

The Market

Now, more than ever, there are market reports and data readily available on the internet. The point here is not to get bogged down in information and to think about your purpose for using the data. Do you want to research market trends, pricing data, what the charity sector themes are, what's happening in other countries? If you are clear on this it will help you to sort for the right kind of information. Sometimes information can come from unexpected market sources. We don't do online training and have no intention of doing so, but reading a report on the growth of online training helped us to see where our differentiation was so that we can be clear about it when talking to clients.

It is also cheaper than ever to conduct your own research. There are all sorts of free survey tools available and online market research companies charge relatively small amounts to do it for you. If you use social media then that can be a great way to spread the news of your survey and get a good level of response. Be clear about your purpose for the survey: the more specific you can be, the more useful the information will be.

There are many other sources of feedback you could use and you can't and shouldn't use them all. Note down which sources of feedback you don't currently use and choose a few to start to bring into your feedback process.

Your Own

One key person in all of this is you. How do you give yourself feedback? Do you give yourself feedback?

How is that little voice in your head? Yes, we all have one, so is it acting like a cheerleader at the side of the field, egging you on and encouraging you, or is it like a scolding parent pointing out all the things you could, should and must do better, making every error a disaster, ignoring any opportunity for a pat on the back?

Whatever the voice in your head is saying, take time to get in touch with what you say to yourself. What feedback are you getting from yourself? Is it helpful? Does it support you? Is it even real? If you aren't sure then ask a trusted friend or colleague and get their take. You can then interpret your own internal responses more accurately. The more emotionally regulated you are, the easier it will be to interpret feedback accurately, including your own internal feedback to yourself. People who are not emotionally regulated tend to distort feedback, either more positively than is helpful or real or more negatively than is helpful or real.

Example

How often have you seen people on *The X Factor*, thinking they are the next Mariah Carey even though they can't hold a note and then berating the judges, saying "What do they know anyway?" On the other hand, how often have you seen the quiet contestant coming in with no idea of their own talent, and even though the judges have all told them how talented they are, they pick up on the things they didn't do well.

We can see this in day to day life (no, *The X Factor* is not real life) where someone has an overly inflated opinion of their ability and ignores any feedback that is contrary to that. And then there is the team member who is overly critical of everything they do, telling you a meeting went really badly, and then they won the contract. They will make small things mean big negative consequences. Either way the internal feedback is inaccurate.

The feedback you give yourself has to be useful. We could argue all day that telling yourself you're a terrible person is useful because it encourages you to always try harder. Notice though how you feel about that feedback – inspired to do something new? We doubt it.

If you've done something well, you don't need to go and shout at the mirror "I'm amazing, get me, what a hero!" – that's just bonkers. You could give yourself a metaphorical pat on the back and decide to do that or take that approach again in the future. When you do something well and it works, doing more of it simply makes sense and you need to be able to develop an ability for accurate feedback for this to be possible.

If you've done something that didn't go well, rather than beating yourself with a massive stick and punishing yourself all day, you could say something like 'That didn't go as well as I wanted it to, what could I do differently next time?' This helps to stop the fight, flight, freeze chemicals from firing and allows your brain to have more choice of behaviour. By giving your brain choice you will be amazed when, the very next time the situation arises, you automatically do something different, because that's what you've programmed yourself to do. Sounds bonkers perhaps, do it anyway and notice the change. John's way of doing this is to say "Genius John, genius" when something happens that is not as planned. It's his way of stopping the fear chemicals running and helping him to stay in the moment and leaves his brain open to more choices. So find a phrase that works for you and use it.

Others?

We've talked about how you give yourself feedback and now we will consider how you filter and sort feedback from other people. Depending on your psychological wiring you will have a preference for how you filter feedback and either look for the 'what I need to do better' stuff or the 'just tell me what's working' stuff. As you are realising from all that you have read so far, each of the preferences has its uses and problems and we discuss these below. As you read this section, if you discover there is a pattern between this and the feedback you give yourself, this is normal because it's the same brain – yours – doing the processing.

'Don't tell me what's good, just tell me what to improve!'

There are some people, you perhaps, who ignore positive feedback and only pay attention to constructive feedback or criticism. They think they are improvement focused. They will tell you compliments are just platitudes. The problem for these people is that they are missing an opportunity to find out what they do well, which means they are not getting an accurate picture of their performance. People who filter feedback in this way often don't even notice the good things that happen; they don't ignore it consciously, they don't even notice it.

If this is you, make it your job to rebalance the feedback you are taking in by making a conscious effort to pick out some positive feedback. WHAT! Yes we know it will be hard and may feel pointless at first; the whole point is continuous improvement – what is life for if not to improve? We get it, and when all you do is look for continuous improvement you can miss the joy of what you are achieving.

Example

A coaching client of ours had been set a particularly difficult sales target to meet and was given two years to achieve it. They worked hard for two years on this and not only delivered the goal early, they exceeded the target set over the two years. A time for celebrating? No, both our client and their boss mumbled a quiet "Well done, glad we achieved it, now we need to do even better over the next two years." So the even bigger target was set and they were off again. Our client couldn't understand why they were feeling tired and unmotivated about the new challenge.

We all, as human beings, need to recognise and celebrate achievements, take time to reflect on it. Constant striving may look good and can bring certain rewards and yet we see so many people who are achieving amazing things and yet never seem to be happy.

Begin by asking yourself 'What specifically do I do well? What am I good at?' By doing this, you will start building a more accurate picture of your performance.

A more accurate picture of your performance will help you to become emotionally regulated, avoid negative overreaction to setbacks and allow you to be consistent and considered in your communication and interaction with other people. As a leader this is essential, if uncommon.

'Just tell me what's working, I don't need the rest' OR 'Don't bring me problems, just bring me solutions'

> ## Myth Buster - Positivity
> Only focusing on the positive is delusional.

There are some people who don't pay attention to any feedback that could suggest something might not be working or needs changing, they are not interested in problems. They think they're just being positive, upbeat and motivational. They are actually being delusional. Here's the newsflash: no one is perfect, it doesn't exist.

By only sorting for evidence of what is working and putting everything (and everybody) else down as moaning or negative, you are missing the opportunity to learn from mistakes and genuinely improve. People will either think you are unrealistic and not on this planet or will keep quiet and hide things that are going wrong. Either way, you will lose credibility as a leader.

If this is you, make it your job to listen carefully to messages you may have dismissed as negative or moaning before. This is not about encouraging negative and unhelpful behaviour; if you feel there are a lot of negative people giving you feedback then probably that's because you are not listening. Instead consider if there are any themes to this feedback which imply a general problem that needs addressing.

The balance between responding to every bump in the road and ignoring the blindingly obvious

Now that you are beginning to get a more accurate picture of what feedback you are hearing, seeing and feeling, what do you do with it? We will talk about this much more in the next chapter when we look at the trait of taking considered risks. For now, begin to think about the balance between reacting to every piece of feedback you get – we call it every bump in the road – and just carrying on regardless.

As with most things, between those two extremes there is the right way for you, and it is different for each of us. Some people will want to keep going for a long time before trying something new and some people will regularly chop and change their strategy even if it takes them away from their key strategic direction. Our question to you is: Is it working? If it is, keep doing it; if not, begin slowly and mindfully to move in the other direction.

In Conclusion

Reading this chapter you will have realised that there is a lot more to feedback than you had previously thought. You've learned what feedback really is and all the sources you can gather feedback from. You've realised that you have a pattern to how you give yourself feedback and where that helps you and where it doesn't and you've also learned you have a preference for how you filter and sort feedback.

We've suggested ways you can begin to develop and stretch yourself using feedback and, like anything in this book, practise, get feedback, practise and develop.

CHAPTER 6

Take Considered Risks

"If you are not willing to risk the unusual, you will have to settle for the ordinary."

Jim Rohn

To do anything in life you need to take a risk. If you never take a risk then you never do anything new, ever. And to be a leader you need to be able to take risks, rise to challenges and make decisions. When you do, you will be seen as a leader who wants to improve things, someone who can communicate and inspire others to grasp the opportunities and a leader whose focus is on doing what others think is impossible.

From our Leadership Study

Quotes in response to the question:

"What aspects of what you do in your leadership position are enjoyable?"

To challenge the status quo and to be the 'foreign element'
Refusing to accept 'ordinary'
Breaking new ground
Making a deal
Getting to put my ideas into action
Making decisions that pay off and feel good

One way in which good leaders differentiate themselves from non-leaders is that to some extent they are prepared to take risks and even enjoy doing so.

As a leader, if you don't take risks you will simply be seen as someone who goes round in circles, tinkering here and there and creating nothing new. Your team will be asked to do more of the same, perhaps in a different colour wrapper, but nothing will change. This type of leadership will lead to stagnation for you and those around you. There are many examples of people and businesses where this is true – which ones come into your mind? One that springs to mind for John is when he was considering changing his career.

John's example

As an accountant for most of my working life, I had learned to play it safe – I hadn't realised how safe until I considered the change. Whilst my career no longer gave me much satisfaction, the fear of changing it was debilitating. I had all the reasons and justifications I needed to stay still: money, house, career, good job, nice people etc. etc. and convinced myself many times that I was right. As a step forward, as I thought at the time, I moved from a safe professional career to a risky (actually still safe) job in industry. Same job, slightly different title and, as you can imagine, I soon became unhappy there too. More reason, analysis, justification kept me there for many more years than was helpful until one day I took a 'sickie'. My first ever. I sat at my kitchen table and looked, really looked, at all the analysis I had. When I was honest with myself and calculated the risk I was taking, I realised that if the worst came to the worst I could make enough money selling chips to keep a roof over my head. That realisation was enough to overcome the fear and I resigned and started my own business.

From our Leadership Study

Quotes in response to the question:

"What would you describe as your keys to success?"

I love getting out of my comfort zone as much as possible

A mixture of fun, realistic outcomes and confidence, maybe a bit of bravery as well

Choosing my battles

I have learned to be more considered

Now notice leaders take 'considered' risks. Not just any old risk without thinking it through, neither do they consider things for ages and then do nothing. Good leaders do both: they take risks and they have a certain amount of consideration about those risks before taking action. The question is: What's the right approach? As with everything, there is no one right way. There are many successful ways to take appropriate levels of risk for you and the context in which you are a leader.

Let's start by thinking about where you are right now.

The All Action Hero

We've all seen them. You may be one of them. Gung-ho, let's go, over the top types who just go for it all of the time and seem to love or be completely unaware of the risks.

And it works – well, sometimes!

And when it doesn't – well, "let's go, over the top... if I keep running fast enough and far enough, the fallout from what I'm doing won't catch up with me!"

The Sloth

Or the other extreme, those people who will not move, take a step or decision until they have analysed it to within an inch of its life, have spoken to 100 people and changed their mind with each person they speak to or be frozen stiff unable to make any decision until it's absolutely clear it will succeed – or not fail, more likely. Is that you? If you're not sure, we suggest you do some more analysis – only joking, it is you!

So which one makes the best leader? Well, neither actually.

Great leaders are driven towards achieving, desire quality and are not scared of failure or rejection. They are not, however, reckless just-go-for-it types either.

In our leadership study, 41% of participants said they look to take action swiftly and 59% said they take time to reflect and consider all the potential issues. It's interesting that, according to the survey, there are more people in the considered category than the more gung-ho category.

As we said at the beginning, if you don't take risks you will achieve nothing. As a baby you could have sat there whilst mum and dad gave you everything you needed and you would have no reason to begin to move around on your own or walk, but you did.

Human beings are programmed to seek more

Why did you have the urge to move? Well, as a baby, you looked around and could see the benefits everyone else had by walking about: the speed they could get from place to place, how they could just go and get things, no need to rely on someone else. So you did it, you took a risk. We have not met a single person in our lives who could walk the first time they tried. It took practice, you fell over but kept going and going until you got your balance and then took your first steps. Even when you fell over after a few steps you didn't give up, you kept practising until eventually you could walk and then run. And then no one could stop you!

So in achieving anything new, you must take the risk that it might not work the first time. Aaaaaaagh! We know, be not perfect, get it wrong. FAIL. We get it. Even worse, it might not even work the second or third time. That was true when you were a baby so what, if anything, is different now?

As a leader, it's healthy to have a committed and passionate attitude about tasks, goals and opportunities and not be afraid of things going wrong. But how do you know the difference between when something is worth continuing to do as practice for future success and when it has failed and no longer worth doing? We talk much more specifically about failure in the next chapter, for now we want to focus on the balance between taking action and reflecting.

In balancing action and reflection you need an ability to understand the risks, assess the consequences and then take action. All the great entrepreneurs and successful leaders we know or have read about in any walk of life have the ability to take considered risks in common. They are not successful all the time, that's not real for anyone, and in the round and over time they get it more right than wrong. Part of this skill involves knowing when to harness their Activist and when to make use of their Reflector.

Activist v Reflector

We all have a preference for either activism or reflecting and like any polarity they both have strengths and weaknesses depending on the context and task at hand.

Activists are action oriented. They get frustrated when nothing seems to be happening. They demand that 'we just do something'. They get a lot of things done, that is their strength and it can also be their weakness. The weakness shows up when lots of action is taken but not on the right things (driving a reflector insane), or when things are quickly dismissed that could have been valuable. A client of Karen's once said "I would rather have a no now than a yes in three weeks' time."

"Really?" was her reply. He meant it when he said it and when they unpacked it he realised that this wasn't a helpful way of thinking.

> **Tips for Activists**
>
> 1. Put a few things off until tomorrow
>
> 2. Take small breaks to think things through
>
> 3. Give a decision 'the overnight test'

Reflectors are natural thinkers, they weigh everything up carefully, think of all the possible consequences and if in doubt, wait for more data. Their depth of understanding and consideration of consequences is a great strength, and a reflector's weakness includes missing opportunities, low productivity (especially in the eyes of an activist) and stagnation.

Whenever John says "Let's think about that," Karen's activist wants to explode! Very often though, for an activist, taking a little more time to consider something makes a world of difference to the outcome (even just a little bit of time, really! – from one activist to another!). On the other hand, sometimes reflectors just need to take some kind of action, even if it feels terrifying and hasn't been studied in enough detail. Our suggestion is when working with a reflector start with something lowish risk or they might implode!

Tips for Reflectors

1. Take some quick decisions

2. Work with task lists

3. Do something, anything

Good leadership requires flexibility

Good leaders see the benefit in both action and reflection depending on the context and issue at hand. The secret is not necessarily to be completely balanced, you always will have a preference and that is also your strength. One useful strategy for leaders is to have someone working with you who you trust and has the other preference. They can be your sounding board, someone to help you slow down or speed up as required.

Taking small steps makes a big difference. Don't ask an activist to go and sit on top of a mountain and consider something – too big a step, it won't work.

For reflectors, their development is to take some quick decisions on relatively unimportant things, like what stationery to pick or what to have for dinner (seriously, they will spend oodles of time on these things!). Task lists can also help you if you are a reflector to get a sense of what needs to be done. We appreciate that if you are a reflector, suggesting that you do something, anything, will send you into a cold sweat. What we mean is that if you are deep in thought about something, interrupt yourself with some activity; it could be completely unrelated to what you were thinking about – go and cut the grass for example. The physical movement can often help you get clarity and encourage you to take action.

Those chemicals again

At the heart of your preference for either action or reflection are your primal biological instincts. Activists are running chemicals of fight or flight, they either attack things or get rid of them quickly. Reflectors are running chemicals of freeze, paralysis when faced with a life-threatening incident. These biological reactions are your inbuilt safety mechanism and you learned them a long time ago for a very good reason. As a result, you will have a lot of processes and strategies in place to ensure you hold on to your preference. Any change to your preference has to be approached carefully, and certainly not by going on a course to learn a new time management model!

Working on your emotional regulation in general will support you in gaining some action with your reflection or some reflection before your action because emotional regulation will stop you from over-responding to your preference, it will just be a preference. When you are emotionally regulated you will have the ability to harness the strengths of the other preference and enjoy the benefits it brings. If at the moment you are rejecting the activist or reflector as just daft, and can't understand the benefits of the other, you need to work on your emotional regulation because you are over-responding and over-fixating on your preference.

The Quest for Quality Reflecting

So now you've worked out where you are on the activist-reflector scale, what do you do? The answer is similar and different for both. If you are more of an activist you need to practise quality reflecting before taking action. You'll be pleased to hear this does not involve staring at your navel for days (let's face it you wouldn't do it anyway); it involves taking time to review and understand the consequences before acting. For a reflector, the issue is action and your development is in your ability to use your reflective time well, then for you to take risks that are considered enough rather than analysed to death.

Whether you are an activist or a reflector, the problem with the quality of your reflecting depends on how you distort risks and consequences in your mind.

Unpicking your distorted thinking about risks and consequences

When you overly distort your thinking in terms of consequences it will paralyse you or lead you to make unhelpful decisions. You will either over distort the negative consequences or underplay them, overly fantasise the possible outcomes or negate them completely. This might seem simple but whether or not you do this well depends on your psychology.

Think about a decision you have made that didn't have a good outcome – how did you assess the consequences?

Do you:

Get overexcited by the positive possibilities and neglect any information to the contrary?

Karen loves George Clooney and used to look at any of his movies and say to herself: "Well, it's got George in it, how bad can it be?" Well the answer, as John will testify, can be 'Very bad indeed'. Karen overly fantasised about the quality of a movie based on the fact that an actor she likes is in it and neglected any other information about the film.

That's a small inconsequential thing (unless you count the hours of wasted time we've spent watching movies we don't like!) but take that out to business and life decisions and people do the same thing. How many marriages are unfulfilling or fail partly because of an overly romantic and unrealistic view of what it would be like? You are living with another human being and no one's perfect, so they cannot possibly live up to those expectations. Personally we partly blame the media and romantic films for this; instead of an age warning on movies there should be another warning that says:

'This film is purely fantasy and in no way represents real life, please just enjoy it as entertainment.'

Do you get hooked into bad business or investment decisions because you get carried away with the excitement of the possible wins? If so, overly fantasising the positives could be your issue. This is what addictive and unsuccessful gamblers do. When you get into this kind of thinking you delete or ignore any evidence to the contrary – that would just spoil it, wouldn't it? We can all do this to some degree of course; after all, wishful thinking makes us feel good. Successful people don't do this often and when they do they learn from it.

Or

Do you catastrophise the negative consequences?

Karen's nan used to say "If you always think of the worst that can happen, you will never be disappointed." She was a master catastprohist! So when Karen travelled to Kenya, her nan would look up all the very worst things that happen or have ever happened in Kenya, as if to prove to her how dangerous it is. Karen is an experienced traveller, she has learned to be sensible and knows that with some planning and due diligence there aren't many places in the world that cannot be navigated safely and enjoyably. Like Karen's Nan, many people distort the negatives to such an extent that they will not move out of their comfort zone. Think about it. If you only think of all the possible negative outcomes of a decision, you will stay paralysed, stuck and maybe just daydream because that's safer than actually doing it. This is because your thinking causes your freeze chemicals to kick in. You daydream from the safety of your armchair whilst justifying why you do nothing.

John recalls a time when he was watching the news with his son Jack when the *Costa Concordia* had just sunk. He asked John: "Does that mean that cruise ships are really dangerous?" He was only five. Many adults do the same and answer their own question. They watch the news and decide that the world is a dangerous place, there are muggers on every street, don't go to [enter the name of any city] or you'll get attacked. John explained to Jack that the reason it's on the news is it's unusual, the news only reports unusual things.

Unfortunately, where people get stuck in their comfort zone they never had that information, for them the news is a reflection of real life. Therefore they don't feel inclined to go out and explore or try unfamiliar things.

When it comes to our own lives we can do the same. We work a lot with people considering exiting jobs, starting new careers, leaving relationships, starting relationships, starting new businesses, moving house, moving country and one of the main pieces of work is helping them to understand the realistic consequences for them of what they are thinking of doing. Not our version of what's realistic, theirs.

These thinking patterns are automatic, you constructed them many years ago and you are rarely consciously aware of them. As a result these thinking patterns happen in a millisecond, so you need to catch yourself thinking it and ask 'Is this real or am I distorting it?' When you can do this you can challenge your own automatic distortions and make decisions with good outcomes by taking calculated risks.

Getting Real on our Distorted Thinking

We're not saying your thinking is wrong. It's not about rights and wrongs. We are asking: Are you checking out your thinking for unhelpful or unreal distortions? By checking out your analysis of consequences more consciously, you will get familiar with your own thinking patterns and identify when they are helpful and when they are not. Then, having done the suggested exercises below, you will automatically begin to stretch the boundaries of thinking and create new choices and options in your mind, thereby creating more flexibility in your leadership style and being able to take more considered risks.

What to do if...
...you over-distort the positive consequences

Think about a time when you were really excited about the possibility of something, really wanted it, went for it and what you got wasn't the outcome you wanted.

Then ask yourself:

1. What information about the situation do you know now that you weren't aware of before you went for it?

2. Thinking back to before you went for it, did you have any sense, thoughts or gut feeling that there was something not quite right that you ignored or didn't check out?

3. Now go back to the point you made the decision to go for it in your mind, with all the information you have just discovered. If you had included this in your original decision making, what would you have done differently?

This process helps you to programme your brain to look for all the relevant information at the helpful point in the process (before you decided to go for it). When you do this a number of times, it will become part of your automatic thinking. The answers aren't always as simple as 'I wouldn't have gone for it'; you may decide you would still have gone for it, and checked out a few more things beforehand or put in some boundaries or caveats that would support you further on.

...you over-distort the negative consequences

Think about something you regret not doing in your life.

Then ask yourself:

1. What specifically do you regret about it?

2. Think back to just before you decided not to do the thing you now regret. How were you feeling? What were you scared of? Were these concerns real or disproportionate given what you know now?

3. What steps could you have taken back then to help yourself look at the situation more realistically? Did you need to talk to someone

who had done it before? Or focus on the positive consequences more? Or talk to someone about your worries and fears so they could have helped you put them in perspective?

This process helps you to programme your brain to look for all the relevant information at the helpful point in the process (before you decided to go for it). When you do this a number of times, it will become part of your automatic thinking. The answers aren't always as simple as 'I would have just gone for it'; you may decide that there were understandable fears or reservations about it at the time and that instead of just dismissing it, you could have decided to revisit it at some point in the future.

It's not for us to say anyone's decision is right or wrong. The only important question is: Are you genuinely happy with the results of it? If you were, it's unlikely it would have popped into your mind during this chapter. Anything that's popped into your mind as you've been reading this is your brain giving you a signal that there was a doubt, or a niggle, or a slight regret about something. Don't ignore this, listen to the message. It will inform your future decisions and improve your ability to take considered risks.

In Conclusion

Now you have read all about taking considered risks and how flexibility around action and reflection will significantly support your ability as a leader to take appropriate risks. As you practise the exercises you develop the ability to evaluate each important situation, taking the right amount of time to consider the options and then acting with clarity and conviction. When you are a leader with clarity and conviction your message is easier for others to understand, align with and act upon.

In the days and weeks ahead, when you are faced with options and decisions to make, remember that taking considered risks allows those around you to feel confident in your leadership and align with you, your communication will become crisp and clear and generate better results more often, and will ultimately lead to the success you are seeking.

CHAPTER 7

Are Forward Focused and Flexible

"I have not failed. I've just found 10,000 ways that won't work."

Thomas A. Edison

We've talked so far about gauging feedback accurately and taking considered risks. All of these great traits lead nowhere if you don't know where you are going. In our leadership research 74% of participants were motivated by achieving long-term goals and 26% by solving complex problems. This speaks to key leadership traits: motivation, attitude to failure and flexibility.

Your ability to become or develop yourself as a leader is based on more than your technical skill in the area you lead. As you have realised already, to become a good leader you need to develop skills in how you think and behave.

In this chapter we are going to apply all that you have already learned about feedback and taking considered risks in our exploration of motivation, forward thinking and your relationship with failure.

The key to great leadership is moving forward with purpose, with clarity of thinking and with the abundant energy required to achieve goals, motivate others and be successful.

Understanding Motivation

In our research, we found that the overwhelming majority of leaders who responded viewed achievement and a drive towards something as a key value for them. This was expressed in many ways including making a difference, achieving great things and making things happen.

From our Leadership Study

Quotes in response to the question:

"What aspects of what you do in your leadership position do you find enjoyable?"

Seeing results and changes
Providing direction, delivering outcomes
Thinking of ideas which are out of the ordinary, refusing to accept 'ordinary'
Coming up with new and different ideas and having the influence and position to make something happen
Being a pebble in a pool to cause positive ripples
Setting the goals and future direction
Breaking new ground, delivering step changes in performance

That ability to be forward focused is not as common as you might think. There is a difference between knowing what you want and actually having the energy and drive to move, sometimes quite slowly and deliberately, towards it. Good leaders have developed this trait. They also seem to be less attached to having only one way to achieve it. Good leaders are flexible and can re-evaluate their progress using feedback, and taking considered risks based on the feedback they get from what people are saying, what they can see happening day-to-day and their own internal feelings of where things are and how they are working.

Adrenalin Junkie?

In our experience of working with many leaders over the years we have found that most of the people (we can't say everyone because we haven't met everyone!) who achieve great things have done so because they were initially motivated to push away from something they didn't want; the key motivation was initially 'to not fail'.

They could have been poor as a child, pushing them to be successful; they may have had a cause they felt passionate about; they might have looked at their parents and thought 'I don't want to be like that'. That motivation, the push away from something, is a strong and essential motivational energy in all of us. It triggers your primary survival fear chemicals of fight or flight which generates the adrenalin to overcome your natural resting state, move forward and do something.

The problem with this strong motivational driver is that if adrenalin runs for too long in your body, it has a negative effect, draining the body of energy. Certain functions in your body may shut down, you can become ill, lose motivation and feel depressed. Not ideal if you are or want to be a leader. Not ideal if you want to be a human being, yet all too often we see this kind of negative consequence in our travels around the world.

We have found that successful leaders at some stage turn their 'push away from' motivation into forward motion; they find something they want to move towards, to achieve and succeed at. The crucial difference in the motivation of moving towards is that it is not adrenalin driven and will not, therefore, lead to the negative side effects mentioned above. The motivation of moving towards is a step-by-step, sustained motivation of keeping going, readjusting as necessary while you remain focused on the long-term goals and outcome. This motivation is harder to keep up than the 'push away from'. The 'push away from' is a strong and sometimes addictive driver; some people even wear Adrenalin Junkie as a positive badge of honour – amazing! We all know drama queens don't we, or people who rush from one high octane and pressured situation to another, back-to-back meetings, fighting fire after fire? John recalls 'I never met Red Adair (shows you my age) though I did see an interview with him. He seemed very calm, I thought, for someone who put out fires for a living'.

Now we have your attention and you have slowed down a bit, there is something we need to talk about! For some of you, perhaps most of you, this may come as a bit of a shock, so if you are not already sitting down, please do so! If you are to achieve the things you want to achieve as a leader, build what you want to build and make a difference in the world, you cannot be afraid of getting things wrong. As part of developing your healthy attitude to being forward focused and flexible, you need to make friends with failure.

Making friends with Failure

"Success is stumbling from failure to failure with no loss of enthusiasm."

Winston Churchill

For some reason, failure is not an exciting or fun word in the English language. The school system doesn't help us on this score. You either pass an exam or you fail.

"Schools and prisons are the only places where time is more important than the job to be done. If I get to New York two hours after you, I have not Failed New York. Yet if I take two months longer than you to learn algebra I have FAILED algebra."

John Bradshaw - *Healing the Shame that Binds You*

You may have learned from your parents that getting things wrong is not acceptable, having been told off when you did. This is not a healthy way to learn and it is endemic in our culture. That a lot of us have fearful feelings about failure is not a surprise. Some people will only attempt things they are absolutely sure they will get right. Not exactly creative or risk taking is it?

What's important is learning to make friends with failure now and letting go of the unhelpful feelings you experience when you think about it.

Karen's example

Many years ago I failed an important exam. I had worked hard and expected to pass. I was devastated. I turned up at my friend's house, in tears, full of self-doubt and shame at having failed something I had been confident I would pass. What would people say? What does all this mean? My friend's husband who had been listening to all this said "Surely the only thing to consider is, is this qualification important enough to you for you to retake it?" That stopped me in my tracks. I had never thought of it like that. He had a history of just having a go at things. His attitude was 'If it doesn't work I just need to decide if I care enough to try again'. It was a strategy that had served him well.

What is Failure?

When you think about it, failure is simply something that didn't work the way, or in the timeframe, you intended. It is no more than that and means no more than that. You only take it personally if your upbringing and life experience has taught you (wrongly) that it is personal and shameful.

Leaders with a healthy attitude to failure are more successful, have more motivated and determined followers, and because they do not lose energy if something doesn't work, have an unlimited drive and energy to keep going and achieve their goals.

Failure is Learning

How would it be for you if it really didn't matter if something failed? Would you become sloppy, lazy and unmotivated? Or would you become more creative, excited and determined? Leaders who think the former are not uncommon. They come from the 'failure is not an option' camp of thinking.

Failure is always an option

If it wasn't an option then no risk taking would take place, ever, and you would never achieve anything new. Is that really what you want for yourself, your business, your children? 'Failure is not an option' leaders rarely achieve anything out of the ordinary. They just do more of the same old thing, though sometimes in a slightly different wrapper which is usually short-lived and not of good quality. Then they move on. Those leaders are motivating people by fear (remember the long-term effects of adrenalin), not encouraging them to become forward focused and flexible. Fear restricts and when you restrict you contract.

Here are some facts about famous failures to help you reframe your attitude to failure. You probably know many of these. Connect with them as you read them:

- Walt Disney was fired from a newspaper for 'lack of imagination' and having 'no original ideas'

- The Beatles were rejected from Decca recording studios who said 'we don't like their sounds' and 'they have no future in show business'

- Oprah Winfrey was demoted from her job as a news anchor because she 'wasn't fit for television'

- Albert Einstein wasn't able to speak until he was almost four and his teachers said he would 'never amount to much'

- JK Rowling was rejected by countless publishers before getting a book deal.

Making friends with failure will lower the unhelpful fear chemicals in your brain and will help you be more experimental, adventurous and become motivated to be forward focused. It doesn't mean you want things to go wrong, it means that you don't set out on a goal or task thinking 'I hope this doesn't go wrong' – that really isn't helpful, remember you get what you focus on. Nor does making friends with failure take away your love of quality and your desire to do a good job. It simply prevents you from being scared and making it personal.

How to make friends with failure

You're now convinced of the benefits of making friends with failure – aren't you? Almost?

To help you get a little more comfortable with it we are going to get you to look at some specific situations with your new eyes and see what you can learn. By practising in this way you will begin to reduce the fear chemicals that used to run and become more emotionally regulated. As a leader this will allow you to feel more in charge of your own actions and move from a 'push away from' motivation to a more creative and expansive forward focused motivation.

Personally

Think about something you would classify as a personal failure. Could be a work project, career, marriage, relationship, house purchase – anything. As you think about it, ask yourself this question and notice what pops into your mind:

If I was to see this event as a blessing in my life, what would the blessing be?

If what pops up is 'not to do it again', please try again! That's you still beating yourself up. The learnings and blessings are much more subtle than that.

Do this exercise on a number of your 'failures' and notice if there is a theme in the blessings. There often is.

In Business

The problem businesses have with failure is the incumbent blame culture. If something goes wrong, the rush is on to find the scapegoat to pin it on, especially in organisations that say 'we don't have a blame culture'.

If you have to say it, it's because it exists. In truth there is rarely one cause of a failure. There are usually a number of interconnected factors which, when you get the learning, really help you to move the business forward. Rarely though do businesses take time to do this, although those that do stand out as exemplars in their field.

Getting to the bottom of it

Think about something that hasn't worked: a project that failed, an important deadline that was missed or a contract you didn't win that you think you should have won.

Use the following process to help you learn from the event, using it as feedback thereby avoiding getting sucked into the blame game.

Process
Get as many of the main participants together in a room, preferably an overheated room with no light and really uncomfortable chairs, shine a spotlight on them... only joking! Get them together and frame that the purpose of the meeting is to ascertain why and how things didn't work out as you all wanted. Using a flip chart or board ask people to shout out all the contributing factors as they see it. As the facilitator, don't allow people to blame other people, keep it impersonal, the focus is on what went wrong rather than who went wrong.

'There was a communication mix-up between systems and marketing' is much more helpful than 'Systems didn't tell us what was going on'.

Once you have all the contributing factors out and with everyone's help, group together the themes and interconnected nature of what happened. This will allow you to see that there were a number of dependent factors at play here (there always are). Once the themes have been identified, stand back as a group and ask "What is this about? Is it about relationships, systems, processes etc.?" When you engage with this process in a spirit of curiosity, you will discover much about what's really going on. You can then decide what action to take rather than who is to blame. Doing this will ensure you dissolve the problem rather than resolve it until it comes round again.

Flexibility

When you have made friends with failure, it frees you up to become forward focused, working towards what you want as a leader.

Definition of Insanity

Doing the same thing over and over and expecting a different result.

The next component of your leadership development is flexibility.

There is no one right way to achieve anything; there is rarely a best way, there are usually a number of equally good ways to achieve something. Good leaders understand this level of complex thinking. The problem is often we each have a different opinion about which way we believe will work. If you have invested all your brain power and energy into deciding this (and you are right of course), why would you want to accept that there may be another way? Good leaders have the ability to hold on to the complex balance of having a clear opinion about something and keeping their brain and ears open for alternatives.

From our Leadership Study

Quotes in response to the question:

"What would you describe as your keys to success?"

Involve the team in decision making – they may not always agree with the way you want to do things
Understand that others have good ideas too
Flexibility of approach depending on the specific situation; I'm able to adapt quickly to different situations without too much discomfort
Going back to basics when the wheels get wobbly
Accepting that it's OK to change my mind and say sorry
I am also flexible and not afraid to alter plans as the project progresses and new situations arise

Many of the leaders in our study highlighted flexibility as one of their keys to success. This is not about flexibility for flexibility's sake, that's just wishy washy. People who hold too many different alternatives can get paralysed and not decide to do anything, so the key as a leader is to develop a favoured path whilst holding in your mind other potential ways, should the feedback tell you that way is not working.

This does two helpful things in your mind. It gives you direction and focus whilst maintaining the confidence that should one way not work, there are other ways to try.

'*Be committed to your outcome without being attached to it.*'

As you have probably already realised, developing flexibility is linked to how we receive and process feedback and how we take considered risks, which is why we're discussing them in this order. If you have no ability to process feedback appropriately or consider risks well, your ability to have true flexibility will be non-existent. As a leader, if you don't have the ability to be flexible, you will find yourself locked into one right way or 'my way or the highway' thinking.

Like all skills and personal development, practice is essential. Below is an exercise we suggest you practise regularly to develop your skill in flexible thinking.

Developing Flexible Thinking

1. Think of something you would like to achieve or have.

2. Write down your initial thoughts as to how to get there. This will be your preferred way for now.

3. Then come up with a least three other possible ways that you could achieve this. If you are finding this hard, go and ask other people. It's amazing what they come up with. Remember you haven't decided yet which one you are going to do, you are just generating options.

4. Once you have four options, decide on your preferred option and hold the others in your mind as possible alternatives. Write them down somewhere if you wish.

Your mind loves choice, and what often happens is that should your preferred way not work out as you planned, the other alternatives will spring to mind, sometimes even adjusted a bit to suit the situation.

Practise this approach regularly and it will become an automatic part of your approach.

In Conclusion

When you combine your skills of embracing feedback and taking considered risks with your increasing awareness of the essential nature of emotional regularity, you have the foundation to develop yourself and become your own style of leader.

Onto this foundation you need to build direction. We talked about motivation, what it is and how it can impact your leadership style and ability to succeed. At some point, whatever 'push away from' you are motivated by, it must be turned around and translated into 'forward focus' motivation. Quite apart from the benefits to your overall health, it is a sure-fire way to lead yourself and others successfully towards whatever your achievements will be, especially when it is combined with your ability to be flexible.

And one final thought for now: How is your friendship with failure going? Early days? Best buddies? Wherever you are in the process, keep going and practise the exercises we suggest and it may help you to add to the list of Famous Failures we've suggested to help motivate you. We'd love you to become a famous failure too.

CHAPTER 8

Do What They Say and Say What They Do

"I had no idea that being your authentic self could make me as rich as I've become. If I had, I'd have done it a lot earlier."

Oprah Winfrey

Good leaders exude trust, believability and congruence. You know where you stand with them. They are clear. You don't even have to like them to follow them and work with them. These leaders are great because they are authentic. They do what they say and say what they do.

Authenticity is one of the most difficult traits of leadership to bring out because it cannot be learned as a skill. It can only come through your own personal development. It's about being uniquely you. Yes, you!

We know, you've spent years creating that perfect image of yourself as a piece of flawless perfection, or the life and soul of the party, or the hard-nosed 'nothing gets to me' type or...? You fill in the blanks for yourself. You then spend a lot of your day-to-day energy living up (or down) to this image lest anyone sees the real you or the cracks in your facade.

We want to see the real you. Only the real you can be a Real Leader. Only the real you can inspire and motivate others. Only the real you can achieve success and healthily maintain it over the long term.

We all put on some sort of facade in life, whether it's meeting someone for the first time, presenting at a conference or looking to impress a date – the old jumper and greasy hair are unlikely to be successful, plenty of time for that later! The issue is not that you created an image; the issue is when the image you project wanders too far away from the authentic you and you have to spend more and more time and energy shoring it up.

Most of us are good at picking up when someone is not quite real even if we don't know exactly what it is. You may have had the experience of the leader, the salesman or the sleazy guy at the bar who said and did all the right things, yet, for some reason, you didn't buy them.

Real Leaders do not do this. They are who they are, they are OK with themselves and that comes across.

Consistent Leaders

The most common qualities which came out as admirable in our study were consistency, honesty and integrity. These are all components of being trustworthy, doing what you say and saying what you do.

From our Leadership Study

Quotes in response to the question:

"Which qualities do you admire in other people?"

The ability to listen, learn and take the occasional knock-back on the chin, before getting back up and pushing forwards with more knowledge, understanding and passion

Being nice to themselves and others

People with courage and integrity

People who give me energy

Trustworthy

Consistency

I can depend on them

Honesty and integrity, perseverance, the ability to communicate and face problems

People who have the humility to accept responsibility for mistakes and who can accept feedback

Being consistent is not about following the same routine every day. It's not about having a standard way of doing something. It's to do with other people's ability to understand you and predict your reactions and behaviour.

Myth Buster - Leading by Example

Leading by example is more to do with your attitude and ability to be consistent, trustworthy and act with integrity than adopting a behaviour because you want other people to copy it or showing people you can do it too.

If you are consistent, people know where they stand with you, and when they know where they stand with you they feel safe around you. When they feel safe around you they are more emotionally regulated and therefore better able to be themselves and use their skills easily.

Consistency is more unconscious than conscious which is why it is impossible to fake. If you are yourself and act how you would instinctively react anyway, you will always be consistent. You will not need to 'work out' every interaction or step to ensure you say and do the right thing.

Karen once worked with a great leader who was brilliantly consistent. When you worked with him, you got a clear sense of his attitude, values and beliefs, because regardless of the context, he was always consistent. Karen was his second-in-command and after going to only a few meetings with him and shadowing him for a few weeks, she was able to represent him in meetings confidently and with authority. She instinctively knew how he would feel about ideas, what his take would be on certain decisions and what kinds of objections he would have. As a result, she needed to escalate fewer issues, could run with projects confidently and felt empowered to do her job.

The benefit for you in becoming a consistent leader is that your life becomes a lot easier – assuming that's what you want? People know you, they know what's important to you – not because you say it, because you demonstrate it. Over and over again. This is what being consistent is all about; it's about what you actually do consistently, not what you say.

Leading by example

This is different from how some people define 'leading by example'. Karen, remembering back to her MBA, recalls a section on leading by example which basically said: 'If you want people to be on time for work, you must be on time for work'. Well yes, but we now know that leading by example is about a way of being as a leader rather than using a set of behaviours because you want other people to copy you. If you demonstrate certain behaviours based on that illustration of leading by example, people will pick it up as fake and you won't be consistent because it is not really who you are.

A leader we worked with did the turning up early and leaving late thing to demonstrate to his staff commitment and discipline. He wanted them to do the same. The problem was he didn't really want to do it; he would rather take his son to school and leave on time to have a nice dinner with the family. Because he resented this, he found himself ducking out of the office sporadically during the day, having long lunches and going to the gym during the working day. He didn't tell his staff this and yet he later discovered many of his staff were doing the same: coming in early and leaving late, but sloping off during the day with all sorts of justifications and excuses. The number of doctor's appointments they had in this business was amazing!

People model your behaviour not your words!

People will model what you actually do, all the time, not what you say. If you pop out to the shops during the day, you are giving them the message that this is acceptable to you. If you are as nice as pie to your superiors but shout at your staff, people will do the same. You can't discipline someone for unacceptable behaviour if you also do it.

Inconsistent Leaders

Inconsistent leaders – I'm sure you know one or two. Sometimes they are interested in the big picture and sometimes they get obsessed with the details. Sometimes they are kind and supportive and sometimes they are punitive and demanding. Sometimes they want you to take them through the plan step-by-step and sometimes they tell you to just get on with it.

You just don't know who you are going to get on any given day. Yes, we all have good and bad days and if you are consistent, people will come to know 'Oh this is one of his not so good days, we know what to expect today'. The unpredictability of inconsistent behaviour is that it puts other people on edge and is likely to fire off their fear chemicals of fight, flight or freeze.

Myth Buster - Keeping them guessing

By keeping people guessing they want them to be keen and motivated to do their best. It actually does the opposite and is all about that person's behaviour and need for control.

Some (not very good) leaders do this deliberately for this reason – they want to keep people on edge. They enjoy the thrill they get of having people run around like headless chickens. These leaders are not emotionally regulated, generally successful, or healthy, for that matter. Their need for control and power is so disproportionate it doesn't serve the needs or goals of the organisation or family. This is never an effective way to lead.

If you are an aspiring good leader though, inconsistent behaviours can be outside of your awareness and the inconsistency may be as a result of who has asked you and if they hit your fear buttons. For example, as a leader you might have one project for a client who you know well and are relaxed with and one project for a client who you really want to impress and don't know well or have heard war stories about. You are likely to behave in completely different ways in these two projects if you haven't developed your own consistent approach.

The art of becoming consistent is in developing your own emotional regulation (yes we know, that again) so that your emotions don't overly drive you, like a demanding boss. You also need to work on developing your own true style rather than overly adapting to what you think other people want.

Honesty

Honesty is more than simply not lying. Honesty is about projecting the same message with your words, thoughts and actions. Honest leaders can express their views clearly without offending other people; this helps people to know where you stand. It also makes you believable.

Myth Buster – Honesty

Anyone who says something hurtful to someone else and then uses the caveat 'I'm just being honest' is engaging in bullying behaviour. There are always ways to deliver even the hardest message without trampling on someone else's dignity.

In our work, if a leader tells us they want their staff to be more honest with them, we invite them to start being honest with their staff. People will not be open and honest with you if you are not with them. You are the leader, it's your responsibility to start this. Not every leader we speak to is comfortable with that idea. That is fine. Simply don't expect honesty from your staff just because you say you want it.

If you are overly concerned with others' opinions, are protective about your reputation or engage in any form of that wonderful corporate game 'Politics', then you are not demonstrating honesty. Any time you have deflected the blame to someone or something else to avoid getting in trouble you are not being honest.

This is why honesty is talked about a lot and not done that well. It's in the pile of 'easier said than done'. You may have good intentions about being honest with people, but your own self-preservation instincts will be pretty strong – and automatic.

It's just like typical exchanges with kids. You see one kid hit another and you ask "What's happened here?" And the response you get is "He started it." Self-preservation. As grown-ups we are not much different, we just have bigger words, longer phrases and an email trail to say 'He started it'.

Being honest is also not about being cruel or unkind about others. You can disagree with someone without tearing their self-esteem to shreds. Anyone who says something inappropriate and hurtful to someone else and then uses the caveat 'I'm just being honest' is engaging in bullying behaviour. There are always ways to deliver even the hardest message clearly without trampling on someone else's dignity. And when someone uses the phrase 'I'm just saying it as it is' they are giving their opinion and missing off the crucial words 'for me' at the end of the phrase.

An honest leader will say that they don't agree with you, and do it without attacking you personally. They will also say if they don't like a decision and be clear if they still intend to execute it and if so why and if not, why. An honest leader will take responsibility for their own mistakes.

A leader who doesn't demonstrate honesty will tell the team at a meeting that they want you all to take more responsibility and ownership, then micro manage the hell out of everything. They will tell you that respect is important to them then publicly humiliate someone in the team. They will tell you that they want to set the strategic direction and will leave the details to you, then bug you with hundreds of suggestions about the minutiae of the project.

Notice we're not calling them dishonest. Most people are not consciously lying. Leaders often believe that it's acceptable to do and say such things, it's all part of being a leader. They may be unaware that their behaviour is giving a completely opposite message and is damaging their credibility.

We can also have positive intentions in our not being honest. A client of ours was talking about an upcoming weekend camping trip away that she didn't want to go on and instead of telling her husband she didn't want to go, she was considering staying quiet because she 'didn't want her kids to not like camping'. Our reflection to her was that surely it was up to her kids to decide whether they liked camping and not her. She realised that in speaking up about her own wants and wishes she was demonstrating to her children that they could express their opinions openly, it actually had nothing to do with camping.

Your staff, colleagues and children will model what you do, not what you say. So if you want them to be honest, you also need to be. Of course you could always use the phrase John's mum uses (as we suspect many parents do): "Don't do as I do, do as I say!" It's a nice try at getting out of it – and it doesn't work.

The art of developing honesty is in becoming less defensive and concerned with impressing other people or controlling situations so you feel OK and is more about your openness to being questioned or even being wrong! We're back to the old issue of failure; making friends with failure will help you to be more honest because it will not hold you in fear the way it did before.

Integrity

Integrity is about living by your principles. Integrity is about thinking through the potential consequences of something you are doing before you do it.

Integrity is not about doing what is popular or doing something in the hope that people will think you are nice.

Myth Buster - Integrity

Leaders with integrity do not always make popular decisions, they make decisions they are prepared to stand by.

The dictionary definition of integrity:

1. Adherence to moral and ethical principle; soundness of moral character; honesty.

2. The state of being whole, entire, or undiminished: to preserve the integrity of the thing.

Looking at the definition, there are a few interesting concepts to explore. The first is the acknowledgement of someone's moral and ethical principles.

We all have moral and ethical principles and they will differ from person to person. One person may have the principle that every person needs to be treated fairly and equally whereas another may accept that the world is not a fair and equal place and sometimes decisions will need to be made where people will lose out. Who is right and who is wrong? They are both examples of equally valid ethical principles. There are no perfect ethical principles, although if you believe in them strongly enough you may believe there are – yours of course.

This is why integrity is difficult to measure. One person may view a behaviour as acting with integrity whereas another may see it as foolhardy, naive or inconsiderate. There will never be an agreed set of ethical principles to live by. Although countless religions try this, individual followers of those religions still have their own interpretation of those principles. What is helpful to you as a leader is to be sure of your own.

The second area to focus on is that in the definition of integrity the first word is 'adherence'. This is important in this discussion because having integrity is not just about having your own set of moral and ethical principles; you have to live by them. We can all pontificate from our dining room table, putting the world to rights, but are we willing to take action, to stand by our principles? Do so even if they might make us unpopular or appear unsuccessful or weak?

John's example

I once worked as a finance director for an organisation. The income was good and I knew I could make a difference, but the way the business was going and some of the behaviours of other people on the board I didn't feel were appropriate for the business and were not supportive of the owner. I felt the owner was being manipulated by a self-serving set of people and was uncomfortable about it. At first I did my best to support the owner and offered a different view, and only when it was clear the owner was too invested in the way things were did I decide to exit the business. This wasn't a popular decision and caused me much short-term inconvenience in lost income, and they did not think well of me, but I was prepared to stand by my decision when it would have been easier to stay, toe the line and take their money.

It's not always easy to stand by your principles. It could even be a great cost to you in the short term. If you choose to stand by a staff member who is being bullied you could become unpopular for 'making trouble' in the organisation. But what if you don't? You are basically sending out the message that you are OK with that behaviour.

This is particularly hard if you are a parent. As the leader of the family you hold the moral and ethical principles of your children's upbringing at heart. If you believe in non-violence and one day your son comes home from school, all proud that today another kid was nasty to him so he punched him, knocked him right over, how do you handle this? It goes against your principles and yet he believes he was engaging in positive behaviour because you've also always told him to stand up for himself.

These are the ethical dilemmas we live with every day. As a supervisor of coaches and therapists, Karen spends a significant amount of time working through complex ethical dilemmas with her supervisees. Confidentiality is important in this field but what happens if someone discloses abuse – a coachee's employer 'just wants to know the gist' of what's going on in the coaching room or a client's partner calls us concerned about their behaviour at home? It's working through the real life issues that puts our integrity to the test.

What's your own ethical code?

The first step is to get clear on your own ethical code. Then you can begin to identify how you can be consistent and honest in line with that code.

To help you develop and become clear on your own code, start by answering the following questions (it often helps to have someone you trust ask you the questions so that you can think freely):

1. If you were to put your purpose in life into no more than three sentences, what would they be?

2. What are you prepared to stand up and be counted for?

3. Why are you prepared to stand up for this? What does it mean to you?

4. What are the beliefs by which you run your life, work life and home life (break them out if necessary)?

5. Where do your behaviours support those beliefs?

6. Where do your behaviours not support your beliefs?

7. What beliefs do you have about yourself, the world and others that you wish you did not have?

8. What stops you from being consistent?

9. When do you find yourself not being honest?

Once you have answered all these questions – honestly of course – identify two or three actions you can begin taking that will help you practise doing what you say and saying what you do.

With practice you will notice a significant change in how you feel day-to-day and also the response you get from others. It will, with practice, become easier and easier to do and the positive results will give you the feedback you need to continue.

In Conclusion

Now you're getting the sense that all of these traits are linked together. To demonstrate being trustworthy you need to have integrity and be honest and consistent. You are probably also getting the idea that it's not easy to be all these all of the time in all situations. That is true for all of us.

With practice, paying attention to feedback and being emotionally regulated, you can do these things and you will be viewed as trustworthy by those who follow you.

Part of the benefit of you developing your own ethical code, being honest and consistent, is that you give those around you and those who follow you permission to do the same. Where trust exists life becomes easier, more fulfilling and rewarding for everyone. There is a risk with this though: you have to stand out, stand up and be you.

This is why developing all of these attributes is not easy and not natural for most people. It takes a commitment to personal development and a commitment to become emotionally regulated. There is no short cut, no quick win on this one. All that is true and what is also true is that when you are a Real Leader, your authentic self, the image you project and the real you are closely aligned. The energetic maintenance bill will be considerably less and your enjoyment of life considerably more.

Doing what you say and saying what you do is not always easy and we have yet to meet a business or leader who has regretted the investment.

CHAPTER 9

Develop Real Relationships with People

"Truth is, I'll never know all there is to know about you just as you will never know all there is to know about me. Humans are by nature too complicated to be understood fully. So, we can choose either to approach our fellow human beings with suspicion or to approach them with an open mind, a dash of optimism and a great deal of candour."

Tom Hanks

Getting Real on Relationships

In Chapter 4 we talked specifically about dealing with problem behaviour in the context of leadership. In this chapter we will be looking at how we develop our relationships in general, not just the problem ones. Why is this important? Well, if your leadership position is your work then you probably spend more time with your work colleagues than with your spouse. Families, far from the superficial rubbish we see on countless twinkly Christmas adverts, are often confusing and far from totally joyous places to be. And even the relationships we hold as near and dear are not like those we see in the movies; as you see from the above quote, not even Tom Hanks is convinced by his own characters.

The ability to build real relationships with other people is a key trait of any good leader. We are not talking about smarm, being nice to everyone or even liking everyone. We are talking about relating to other people in a way that respects both of you and helps you move towards your goals.

Myth Buster - Perfection

No-one is perfect. Don't expect perfection from yourself or others, you will never find it.

So if you're reading this thinking all your relationships are perfect and you don't need to improve or develop your relationships in order to be a good leader, then self-awareness may be your issue!

From our Leadership Study

Quotes in response to the question:

"In the context in which you are a leader, what is important to you? What drives you?"

Seeing other people achieve and develop
Good morale within team
Seeing people flourish
Successful team
Helping others to achieve their potential
Respect
Building good relationships with my staff and peers
Being fair
Teamwork
Seeing others grow and develop

In our leadership research, the relational aspect of leadership was something that participants rated as very important and a key driver for them.

This is unsurprising and encouraging; without people who follow you, you would not be a leader, not a good one anyway. The leaders in our survey were generally very focused on people and relationships, many of their key problems and challenges were related to people. A lot of what they loved about their work was people-focused. In areas of development, many participants cited relational aspects of their position as development areas.

From our Leadership Study

Quotes in response to the question:

"What are your main areas of self-development at the moment?"

Challenging challenging people
Further development of courage to challenge
Being more assertive in my own self-achievements and capabilities within the workplace
Patience
Being a more rounded person
Being able to express emotions more freely
Thinking before I speak! Can be too upfront about my opinions and not good at considering the sensibilities of my audience
Being aware of staff issues
Being approachable
Taking things less personally

Good leaders are constantly working on the relational aspects of their position. They know no one has ever really got relationships sorted. As we change and our world changes, the quality of our relationships is ever more important.

Having a real relationship means there is a psychological contract between two people. This is my role in your life and this is your role in my life. Sometimes these are obvious, sometimes they aren't. When you visit the doctor your contract with him is concerned with your health – he does his part, you do yours. This is why many people find networking events a bit of a joke; far from being an opportunity to find real reciprocal relationships which can be mutually supportive, they become a business card flinging match, followed by many sales emails no one wants to receive. Good networking organisers have now grasped the concept of fostering real relationships in networking which is beginning to generate real results.

You will have noticed the concept of real relationships has been a key component through much of this book and is threaded through most of the other chapters. In this chapter, we will look specifically at responsibility in relationships, how you take your share of that responsibility and how you can develop your own relationship style that is true to you. When you can do all this your relationships will become smoother, easier and more enjoyable in whatever context you operate as a leader.

Responsibility in relationships

Think about this:

In all of our relationships, we are 50% responsible for the relationship and we are 100% responsible for our 50%. As human beings we are equal, no one is more or less than the other – now there's a thought!

This might seem idealistic as a concept, we get that. What we are suggesting is that if you want to be a good leader, and want people to follow you, developing and maintaining good relationships will make life easier. If the concept is still a little difficult to grasp, read on. It will become clearer and remember we are not talking about skills or intelligence here. One person may be more capable or less capable at a certain task than someone else. Here we are talking about how we view each other as people. You are always OK, your skills are another matter.

We have our half and they have their half, that sounds fair, doesn't it? Now ask yourself 'Do I believe that?' And if so, do you believe it and do it? It seems like a simple statement, and it is; the complexity comes when you start applying it to real situations. Let's look at this in a bit more detail.

More than 50%

Some people take more than their 50% responsibility for the relationship. They deny the other person their responsibility for the relationship. You will hear them say things like 'they won't know what to do if I'm not there' or 'they can't cope without me'. They see themselves as more than the other person.

Less than 50%

Some people take less than their 50% responsibility for the relationship. They deny their own empowerment and give power to other people. You will usually hear them say things like 'well they know best' or 'I never get it right anyway'. They see themselves as less than the other person.

Control and Accountability

Look at relationships in terms of control and accountability. If you expect other people to read your mind or fall in line with you, you are not taking responsibility for your 50%, you're putting more of the responsibility on to the other person to do something. On the other hand, if you expect people to mess up or forget things, you are taking responsibility for some of their 50%, you are assuming they are less than you and can't do something unless you take control.

We're hearing some of your minds going 'Well, that's all well and good and makes sense to some degree, BUT what about as parents with children or positions of authority, surely then I do have more than a 50% responsibility?'

Well actually no, we are talking about **responsibility** for the **relationship**, not the **task** in hand.

Parent and child

If you are a parent, you have the responsibility of bringing up your child, keeping them safe and supporting the growth of their self-esteem as much as you can. The child has a responsibility to grow and learn about how to get on in the world. Most of this is fortunately biologically programmed at birth. So the parent has their part to play and the child has their part to play – each has their 50%.

Let's look at this using an example:

Imagine you are playing with your child and you are down with them on the floor, letting them guide the play, telling you what shapes to find and build with the Lego as part of their game or telling you what to draw, asking for help as and when they need it, and simply being there with them. In that situation you are probably doing your 50%.

Imagine now that you get down on the floor and you help by building all their Lego for them or colour in all the drawings. In that situation you are probably doing more than your 50%. We understand that you believe you are showing them how to do it right (yes, that good old word 'right'!) but children are naturally designed to explore and discover, they will work out how things fit together, how to draw a picture, in their own way, with some guidance from you, not you showing them how you do it your way.

Beginning to get the complexity and subtlety in this?

Position of Authority

If you are a leader in business, the other people who work with you are still adults – we heard that, yes they are! You may have more responsibility for the outcome or project but you all have your own 50% responsibility for the relationship. So do you run around after your team, designing endless processes to keep them on track, mediating lots of discussions just in case there's a problem? If you do, you are disempowering them by taking more than your 50%, regardless of why you believe you have to do it. Alternatively, do you give them the 'rope to hang themselves with', withdraw support so they can learn 'the hard way' or deflect key leadership decision to the team in the interests of 'democracy'? Then you are deflecting responsibility by not taking your 50%.

These are subtle differences which can transform or destroy a team.

We are not saying this is easy. Why do you think it's the second to last chapter? We are saying it is important. The reason most people find this so hard is to do with their own upbringing and life experience, the perceptions of power and control they learned in their families for example. This stuff can be quite hard-wired in you, and the good news is that it is possible to change this wiring and allow you to have real relationships where everyone has their own responsibility and appropriate level of empowerment.

If you are beating yourself up at this moment for being a bad parent or bad leader, stop it, it doesn't help. Trust us, we've been there. Go back to Chapter 6 and remind yourself that the first step is awareness. When you use your awareness as feedback you can decide what, if anything, you want to do differently.

Making it real

To bring this to life a little more for you, think about some of your key relationships. Do you take more than your 50% or less than your 50%? It's not statistical answers we're after, it's a general sense. Which side of the see-saw do you normally hang out on? You'll probably find there is a pattern. Once you have the pattern, look at the people you have around you, either at work or home or socially. Because we naturally attract the people we need in our lives, you will find that whatever you do, your staff or life partner does the other. If you take more than your 50% of responsibility for relationships, you will naturally find other people who take less than their 50% of responsibility for relationships. That's how it works and is not necessarily something most people are aware of until they look.

So now you have this awareness, how do you own your 50% of the relationship and give the other person their responsibility? You do this by becoming assertive not aggressive, supportive to others without rescuing them and vulnerable not a victim. You learn to take responsibility for yours and let other people take responsibility for theirs.

Assertive rather than aggressive

When we see aggressive behaviour from someone, it is an attempt to be 'more than' the other person. They are coming from an attitude of 'attack is the best form of defence'. When someone needs to put the other person in their place (i.e. down) that's when they behave in an aggressive way. We talked about this in Chapter 4 when we were discussing bullying behaviour. Bullying is an extreme form of aggressive behaviour. For most people aggressive behaviour comes out because they are not emotionally regulated and have not learned to be assertive. As a result, their best attempt at being assertive comes out clumsily as aggression. Aggressive behaviour is a bit like when a little child or teenager throws a tantrum; in many ways that's what happens for people when they do this. They go back to being two or fifteen, literally in their mind, and behave as a two-year-old or stroppy teenager. How many tantrums have you seen from supposed grown-ups in a meeting? Or, dare we ask, how many tantrums have you had (all justifiable, we understand) and left the meeting thinking 'Why on earth did I do that?' We see it often in the training room and the boardroom; it's interesting watching an adult behaving like a child and trying to justify it with big words and logic. Not that we have ever done such a thing!

The problem is that, particularly in a fear-led culture, these behaviours can sometimes frighten other people and you may, wrongly, think that the aggressive behaviour has created the result. Then you think 'Well that got me something, I'll do that again' and that's where the trouble starts. If aggressive behaviour got you nowhere, you wouldn't do it. And it's worth noting that often the person doing the behaviour is not consciously aware of it.

Being assertive is more to do with your emotional regulation, your attitude and your view of the other person than the specific words you say.

If you have too many anger chemicals running in your brain, you are likely to have low self-esteem and believe that in order to feel OK you must get above the other person. In that case, a question like 'How do you think that helps?' will come across as judgmental and sarcastic. If you have emotional regulation and see the other person as an equal human being, you will say it with different energy, tonality and purpose.

The problem for many people is that they don't speak up early enough when they are not happy about something, so it builds and builds and then comes out with a whole bucket of frustration behind it. Some people are also out of practise at doing, or have never really done, conflict healthily. We would go so far as to say most families do not do conflict well, as a way of expressing views and feelings and working towards a solution. For most families you either 'don't fight in front of the children' which does nothing to help them develop assertiveness, or everyone shouts, screams and strops around with no respectful resolution. Then years later the very same behaviour turns up in the boardroom!

So if this is your area of development (ask a friend if you are not sure – they will be), work on your emotional regulation and get practised at being assertive. We're not suggesting the first thing you do is go straight to your partner and give them a list of all the things you think are not working in your relationship that you haven't had the courage to speak up about until now. Please don't – it won't end well!

You have to practise first. Start with smaller things like complaining in a restaurant or taking something back to a shop. One of the best ways to practise is dealing with cold callers. Your challenge – should you choose to accept it – is to get them off the phone whilst maintaining everyone's dignity and not getting angry. It's a challenge but it's great practice. The key is to practise in a low-risk environment and build up gradually as your brain and emotions get used to it.

Practise the process below to help you develop your assertiveness:

1. Think about the message you want to give. It could be your dinner is cold, this dress has a hole in it or you don't understand why you have been given that project.

2. What's the outcome you want? A fresh meal, your money back, to gain understanding?

3. Focus your attention on remaining calm and holding the other person in your mind with respect.

4. As you speak, outline factually what has happened and what you would like to have happen as a result. Deliver this authentically and in language natural to you.

Below are some examples of the phrases you could use for the earlier examples:

'My dinner is cold, could I have a fresh one please?'

That's clear and much more helpful than prodding your dinner with disgust and ranting on for five minutes about it.

> *'This dress has a hole in it, I would like a refund please.'*

Again you are being clear about what you want the other person to do – better than giving a long story about you wore it to a party and it was so embarrassing and the quality is disgusting, blah blah blah.

> *'I'm confused as to why you have given me this project, could you take me through your thinking on it please?'*

This will help you gather information and generate discussion which will be more beneficial than going on and on (and on) about how busy you are, it's not really your department anyway and 'so-and-so' hasn't much to do so they could do it!

Get the idea? Being assertive is about being clear, not venting your anger. The anger comes because we're not emotionally regulated and have let something build to a point where it just bursts out. You will know if you've been assertive rather than aggressive because the other person will respond as a grown-up, not shrink into their shell or flip out like a child.

It is particularly important to say what you would like to have happen so that the other person knows specifically what to respond to. But we don't want to do that, do we? What if they say no? Then we'd feel either rejected or indignant, depending on where our excess of unhelpful chemicals is. Difficult as it may be at the beginning until you have had more practice, this development is an essential part of owning your 50%, not expecting others to read your mind – you need to be clear.

Supportive rather than rescuing

I'm sure you all know one or two of them: the rescuers! They don't exactly arrive in the office with a red cape and their underpants outside their trousers but they may as well. They want to help – in fact they want to do everything. They would even write your emails for you because you are obviously too stupid to think for yourself! An exaggeration, maybe. Like aggressive behaviour, rescuers also come from a position of thinking they are 'more than' other people, so they must save other people from themselves. They don't say this of course, they are way too nice. They are 'just being helpful' i.e. patronising and 'want to support the team' i.e. get thanks for saving the day. We've heard it all.

The problem is if you are doing more than your 50% you are rescuing not supporting.

You are not empowering others, you are taking away their power. You know you are rescuing when:

- You take it upon yourself to do something for someone else without asking them if they actually want it.

- You do something for someone else and you are wanting, hoping and maybe even expecting thanks or gratitude.

- You feel a sense of power, authority and purpose when you are 'helping' others.

- You say to yourself or others phrases like 'they couldn't do it without me', 'what would you do without me?', 'it's just as well I'm here'.

And as you read this, it is important to realise that this behaviour is mostly unconscious, we don't go around thinking 'who shall I rescue today?' Well, most of us don't, anyway. If your preference is to rescue, the chances are you learned it as a child, when you were rewarded for being a 'good boy' and 'sharing your toys with others' or helping Mum, and this reward and recognition pattern develops until it becomes your adult habit. The problem with rescuing is that you are not really helping the other person, you are denying them the opportunity to help themselves and you are probably neglecting your own needs.

When you watch the in-flight safety demonstration on a plane, they always say "Put your own oxygen mask on before helping others." There's a reason for this. If you are dead you can't help anyone and all rescuers need to apply this principle in their lives more.

Example

A coaching client of ours was talking about how five of the team of seven were currently off sick with one thing or another. Rather than look at why this was the case, the client was explaining how he was worried about the other two members of staff and was trying to do as much as he could to take workload away from them to reduce their stress. It came as a complete shock to him when we asked what would happen if he became ill.

Karen watched a TV programme about food poverty recently where a mother couldn't afford to feed herself and her child, so she lived on cups of tea all day whilst making sure the child got fed nutritious meals. Now if you are a natural rescuer you'll probably be thinking that's a wonderful mother. Think again. As the chef who was helping this lady pointed out, if the mother didn't look after herself and became ill, what would happen to the child? The woman's response was amazing, she had never thought of it like that before and it was all the motivation she needed to change her attitude and the chef taught her how to make them both nutritious meals on a small budget. A simple and powerful shift of thinking and behaviour that will support both of them.

If you want to move away from rescuing to supporting others, here are things that you can do to help you make the change:

- Work on the emotional regulation of your guilt or shame feelings.

- When you feel that you are just about to step in and take charge of a situation, stop. Then ask the other person if they would like you to help them. If they say yes, ask them what specifically they would like you to do. This empowers them whilst offering your support. If they say no, leave them alone!

- Practise, practise, practise asking people **if** they would like your help. When you see someone who looks like they are struggling it will tug on your rescuer cords, but sometimes people are not actually struggling. And if they are, it will be part of their development (see victim behaviour below), to ask for help when they need it.

- Start looking after your own needs more. This is not about spending all weekend at the football rather than with the kids, or going to a spa for a week. Make the change in small, manageable steps, taking small chunks of time out, to read a magazine, take a long bath, or head off to the park to get some quality strategic thinking space. When at home, negotiate this with your partner so you both have opportunities to do this. It will do wonders for you both, be much easier than you think and it will be a great example to your children in supporting them to take care of their own needs. Yes, we are back to leading by example again.

Vulnerable rather than a Victim

Vulnerability is a sign of strength. If you don't believe this, then this part of the book will be important for you.

When a leader can be vulnerable, they have made friends with failure and have emotionally regulated their fear and sadness chemicals. Putting on a brave face is just covering up your fear or sadness. We're not saying that as leaders you need to go around sobbing with team members because their budgie died or crying out in fear as the sales figures fall into your inbox. Being vulnerable is about being human.

People often get confused between vulnerability and victim behaviour. This is not surprising because demonstrating vulnerability is not that common, often as a result of being told or modelling from others that vulnerability is a bad thing, a sign of weakness. John is from the west of Scotland so being vulnerable is dangerous, let alone a weakness! The favourite phrase there is 'get over yourself' which is really helpful. The west of Scotland has one of the highest alcohol dependencies and heart disease problems in the western world.

Victim behaviour comes from a position of thinking that you are 'less than' other people. Victims are taking less than their 50% responsibility. If you are performing a 'good victim' role you will want other people to take over, because you're just useless. Victims often feel picked on or persecuted by other people and will spend a lot of time moaning about other people, their partners and life in general. They aren't interested in what they can do to help themselves, they want other people to help them or pity them.

We want to be clear about the difference between victim behaviour and being a victim of, say, bullying, for example. There is a difference. We have sometimes seen leaders shirking their responsibility in bullying situations by telling the person being bullied to stand up for themselves or pull their socks up. Yes, it can help a victim of bullying to become more empowered and develop assertive behaviour; as the leader, however, you still need to deal with the bully. Victim behaviour on the other hand is a behavioural pattern of feeling generally 'less than' most people. These individuals are usually consumed with their own self-pity and the woes of the world. They won't be the office ray of sunshine!

Being Vulnerable

The key difference between victim and vulnerable behaviour is in what you expect other people to do. When you are being vulnerable you do not expect anyone else to do anything with it, you are simply expressing how you feel without expecting anyone to save you or attack you. When you are vulnerable you can say 'I'm upset about that' and not expect everyone to rally round with cakes and sympathetic ears (i.e. joining with you in your patheticness). If you are being vulnerable sometimes you have to tell people, especially the rescuers, that you just want to talk about something and you don't want them to do anything with it. Being vulnerable supports constant emotional regulation because you can say 'This is how I feel' without having any agenda or expecting anyone to take action, give sympathy or beat you up. Vulnerability takes strength because someone who is not emotionally regulated and running too many anger emotions (the aggressive person) will see vulnerability as an opportunity to get one over on you. When you are vulnerable you have the strength to hold them to account for their behaviour, whilst remaining open. Holding them to account could involve taking them aside and explaining that you thought their comment was inappropriate, or if they do it to everyone in the team, you might choose to explain this publicly. That will show others both your strength and vulnerability, demonstrate to them that this type of behaviour is unacceptable and provide them with a leadership role model of how to do it. The main thing in such a situation is to remain calm and not get hooked into explaining or justifying yourself in any way; that will only play into their game.

If you are prone to a bit of victim behaviour, and let's face it, we all do it now and then, here's what you can do to turn that into vulnerability.

- Work on your emotional regulation of your sadness and fear chemicals.

- When you are tempted to have a moan about something, ask yourself 'What is my intention in doing this?' If you want to talk something through with the aim of finding a way forward, that's not victim behaviour. If you want to have a good old moan about things to make yourself feel better, save it for the pub.

- Begin to think about ways in which you can support yourself. For example, next time you are looking to make those sad eyes at your partner and say "I feel thirsty" in that whiney voice, stop yourself and either say "Could you get me a drink please?" or get up and do it yourself.

- Begin to train your mind to think in more empowering ways. When a negative thought drifts into your mind, ask yourself 'What, if anything, can I do about this?' You will then start to consider what you can do and what's outside of your control.

Each Role Needs a Friend

You may notice that these roles are connected with each other in their less helpful forms. Every victim needs an aggressive person to pick on them and someone nice and helpful to rescue them from the bad people. Every rescuer needs victims to rescue and 'those' aggressive people that they can save the world from. Every aggressive person needs a victim to pick on, a rescuer to ridicule.

These roles are the basis of every superhero movie, soap operas, politics and generally every walk of life.

The issue with them being so commonplace is you could be led to believe that is the way the world is, that is how to behave and that all you do is choose which role you prefer to play. Whilst common, this game is unhelpful to everyone involved in it. As a Real Leader in the Real World we want you to stop playing the game, step into your own life, take responsibility for what is yours and allow other people to have their own responsibility.

You will also have noticed, as you read about the three behavioural roles, that you can be performing two or even all of them in their less helpful forms at times. The good news is that this makes you human, we all do these things at times, it's normal, though unhelpful for you as a leader. As a leader you need to step out of and beyond these games.

Begin by getting awareness of the regular games you play. Think of specific situations and look at the circumstances and other people involved when you fall into each one of the roles. As you think about the situation, notice how you felt, what hooked you in, what were you trying to do and how did it end? When you pay attention to what is going on it will help you be specific on your development of each of these areas and what you need to practise.

By becoming assertive, supportive and vulnerable you are giving permission to and inviting other people to do the same. They may not, and they may well escalate their behaviour to try to get you hooked into your old behaviour.

We worked with a great lady who was a 'rescuer leader' to her team of victims, saving them from all the nasty bad clients. When she learned the different roles and their more helpful opposites, she decided to change and worked on her assertiveness and supportiveness. She was looking to empower them and help them to work through their communication issues with clients. To her shock she found they just got more and more needy at first. There were tears at dawn and then they all turned on her saying she was a bad leader. They wanted the nice rescuer back.

Sometimes people don't realise you are trying to help them; they got something out of the other way of behaving, so why change? This may happen initially and keep going; eventually it will work its way through and then you'll have an empowered, motivated team. It does take some work and tenacity though, but those qualities are not lacking in good leaders, and it will ultimately take much less energy than continuing with the old way.

In Conclusion

Developing real relationships takes time, discipline and awareness. Good leaders know that the key to their success is in building and maintaining these relationships and they take the time and make the effort to do it.

If you have a relationship issue with someone, you are part of the issue and so are they. Your development as a leader is in taking your 50% and allowing other people to have theirs.

PART 4

DOING IT
IN THE
REAL WORLD

CHAPTER 10

Stepping Out into the Real World

"I think there's some connection between absolute discipline and absolute freedom."

Alan Rickman

Many people tell us they know things. This usually means they don't do it.

Awareness, knowing things, is only the start. To become a good leader you need to do more than know things; you need to take action using your knowledge. Congruent, consistent and real action. Using the latest buzz words, saying the 'right things' and paying lip service to them is not the same. People see through it. It is amazing to us how many businesses do all of this and then wonder why they still have issues.

A client of John's recently commented on how they could not believe that given that people costs are the most significant part of the business costs, the board 'say all the right things in public and take actions and do behaviours that undermine their staff rather than utilise their great skills and energy'. It astounds us as well.

Having read the book we invite you to consider what you want to do, want to learn or change to develop your leadership skills. You see, without behavioural change there is no learning. Therefore unless you change your behaviour you will have learned nothing.

Our aim in writing this book was not to drown you with psychological theory or clever new models. We wanted to write something that was enjoyable, interesting to read, made sense and has practical application. Ultimately for us, the point of this book is to provide you with things you can actually go and DO something positive with.

If you look at the comments from our leadership study throughout the book, you will see that most people, like you, are inspired by honesty, integrity, developing people and being successful. The leadership study also showed that people do not like bullying, arrogance and falseness. The very fact that they are saying this in the study is because it exists, all too often, in the world even today.

We need a change of approach in this world and we want you to become a Real Leader and help make that change. The more Real Leaders there are, the more people will be encouraged and supported to be their best, live a more fulfilling life and have less stress. We see far too many leaders and potential leaders following the same old pattern of leadership: the tough, 'it's a jungle out there' type of thinking that belongs to the past and yet is still very much alive and well in the present. We want you to begin to make the change that is needed. It sounds like a cliché and it is true. Change is not made by large organisations or governments. It is made by individuals changing the world around them for the better. You know how you felt when you experienced bad leaders – don't be one of them. You do not need to behave like them to get on and be successful.

Developing yourself as a Real Leader in the Real World includes having the discipline to keep practising, refining and improving yourself. We mean discipline in terms of being disciplined in your approach, not beating yourself up if you've not done all the exercises in this book, if you forget some of the concepts or even if you've not read all the chapters. Throughout this book we have emphasised that we are all different and that you need to become your own style of leader, and therefore you will each take different things from this book.

You, as a leader, have to become your own guide of your own development; no one can make anyone learn anything and that includes you. To learn something you have to be motivated to learn, see the benefit in the learning and believe that it is possible to do. It can be a stretch for sure, and you need to know that you can do it, to do it.

Discipline

Definition:

'Activity, exercise or a regimen that develops or improves a skill.'

Discipline is the development of a new habit, one you choose to develop, not that you are told to. Having a disciplined approach is not easy because it takes repetition to install a new habit. Like exercise or a healthy diet, you don't get fit or lose weight by going to the gym once or eating lettuce for one day. You need a plan, a programme, a way to create a new discipline which will help you to achieve your goal.

If you've read this book, we think it's safe to assume that you have a goal to be the best leader you can be, to be steps ahead of those who've swallowed the latest leadership theory, to be real with those around you and enjoy flourishing relationships. You probably also have a goal of having a rich, fulfilling life that encompasses your work. We assume this because if you were simply looking to get through each day until the weekend, the next Christmas, or the next trip to Majorca, you wouldn't even have picked this book up. For you, life is more than that. So do you have the discipline to go ahead and make the changes you need to get there?

If the answer that comes back from your head is no, or not now, that's OK. We have often read a book the first time to get a sense of it all and then come back later, sometimes even many years later, and begun to work through it. Karen recalls "Covey's 7 Habits of Highly Effective People I thought 'interesting, not sure what to do with all that though' and put it back on the bookshelf. At the time I didn't have the experience or the motivation to put his principles into practice. When we started up Monkey Puzzle it was the first book that popped into my head. My brain had stored it away somewhere just ready to bring to my attention when the time was right".

If the time is right and you are ready, then begin by deciding where you want to start your development. People do this in different ways. There is no one right way. We haven't structured this book in the order you need to do things, we structured it so that the concepts and ideas in each chapter build on the former chapters. So start where you want to and with what fits best with your style of learning.

If you noticed a theme for you as you've read the book then perhaps start there.

It could be to focus on improving your emotional regulation generally as that will give you a good solid foundation to build the other traits.

Perhaps you have pressing problems? If so, use this book to help you address these to begin with.

Have you recognised traits you don't have or show less well as you read about them? Then it makes sense to start with them.

And if you simply want to practise some of the ideas in a step-by-step way, in a safe environment, then try them out and get feedback before you go further.

The key is to get started!

The sooner you begin, the quicker you will get the results that will give you the confidence and motivation to continue.

Develop your discipline of self-development, create your new useful habits and they will be the key to your freedom.

Freedom

Definition:

'The power or right to act, speak, or think as one wants without hindrance or restraint.'

Hang on! Back up there a minute! How can discipline lead to freedom? Isn't discipline about sticking to something, restricting yourself, controlling yourself and freedom is to do with being expansive and having lots of choice? Well yes, to both. And now you can see from the definitions of both that they are not mutually exclusive.

We know that some people can see discipline as something restrictive, especially if your experience of life has taught you that. Yet if you don't make a decision to do something, and have the commitment to work towards it, how can you ever have freedom? All the choices and expansive thinking in the world won't result in anything if you remain as you are, doing what you've always done, the same way you always have. That sounds more restrictive than deciding to make a change.

Freedom requires belief in yourself, belief in others and the realisation that we all have choices and the right to exercise those choices. There are leaders who seek to control other people, what can be said, how it should be said and what is right and wrong. This is not leadership, this is control.

Good leaders know this and employ skilled and inspired people and create the structure and environment to support them. We are not talking anarchy here – heaven forbid – we are talking giving others, and yourself, the freedom to develop ideas and concepts, find new, better more efficient ways to achieve things.

As a leader looking forward, ask yourself what you say to yourself when you look at your team, family or organisation. What do you see around you? How do you feel? Is your urge to control, make sure things don't go wrong, that mistakes aren't made? Are you saying 'Yes, great idea but we need to be careful of....?' If this is you, what will happen if you let go, just a little, of the need to control? What could be achieved if you see your role as creating and communicating the overall direction and vision and allow others to use their time, energy and skills to generate the ideas and actions to get you all there?

Freedom can be scary. We get that. It is also empowering, liberating and inspiring. If you are feeling restricted in any way right now, ask yourself why. What is really happening and what can you do to release yourself?

Modelling

One important way to help and support your own leadership develop is to model leaders that inspire you. And we mean model them, not copy them. It's essential you are yourself and not a clone of someone else.

Begin by thinking who are the people that inspire you, your role models, the people you follow or would be happy to follow if they were leading.

Make a list of them. They can be people you know personally and can talk to, people you see and can observe or even people you can only read about. Once you have your list, take one at a time and begin to observe what it is about what they do that you like and respect. We want you to model **what** they do, not **how** they do it. How they do it is their style, their way, not yours. Focus on what they do. For example, do they spend more time listening than talking? What do they do at the start of a meeting? What key things do they focus on?

Once you have a sense of some of what they do, practise. Work out how you can, in your own style, do something similar and then take the feedback. It's not about taking everything they do, that's copying.

It's about identifying what works for you, what when tweaked slightly works for you and what doesn't work for you.

As you get going with your modelling notice:

- If something stands out as an essential trait that someone has that will help you immediately then start there.

- Is there a common trait that all the leaders you admire have? If so perhaps you start there.

- Is there an inspiring leader you know that you can talk to to get ideas?

Having read the book, what inspiring leadership traits do you now realise you already have? Where else can you use them that you hadn't thought about before – at work or at home, in the community? Or, now you are aware of your skills, will you use them more often and more consciously?

Emotional regulation

The key to being a Real Leader, as you learned in Chapter 2, is to be emotionally regulated. It is the foundation of all healthy, consistent, congruent and inspiring leaders.

When you are an emotionally regulated leader you will be able to make better choices about how you spend your time, and interact with rather than react to other people.

Emotional regulation will allow you to receive and accurately interpret the feedback you are getting then act appropriately based on it. Taking calculated risks will become easier and less stressful as you will not be reacting based on fear and this, in turn, will allow you to look to the future and focus on all that can be achieved.

With that strong foundation you will provide clarity to those around you and they will know that you mean what you say and they can rely on you to follow it through.

And with all of this you will engage with other people from a place of mutual responsibility for what is now and what needs to be done.

There are many ways to implement the concepts in this book, develop the discipline you need, reach your own freedom and become a Real Leader in the Real World. We suggest that after reading the book through once, you then use it as a reference tool, re-reading chapters as they become relevant to what is happening for you at the time.

When something is not quite where it needs to be, ask yourself what is going on. Do you feel that you are calm and reacting appropriately, or have the fight, flight or freeze chemicals come out to play? Which of the age old problems is creating the issue or pressure for you and you need to refresh your memory on? Or, which of the five key behaviours are you not doing in the way that will get you what you want?

Taking it out into the Real World

However you start, wherever you start, all we ask is that you start.

Begin by asking yourself:

Where will you start?

Which disciplines do you want to develop in your life?

How often will you review your progress?

How will you know you've achieved them?

Just because it has been the way it has in the past does not mean it has to be that way in the future. We're committed to supporting the growth of Real Leaders in this world, to inspire you to step out of the shadows, be yourself and lead.

From our hearts to yours, we wish you all the best in what you do.

Karen & John

About the Real Leaders for the Real World Programme

The Real Leaders for the Real World Programme is a six-month programme designed for leaders from business, the public sector and community leaders.

In the programme, Karen and John work with the group and with each participant individually to support them to become a Real Leader. The course covers in depth:

- The Age Old Problem of Time
- The Age Old Problem of Other People
- Using Feedback to Succeed
- Taking Calculated Risks
- Becoming Forward Thinking and Flexible
- Do what you Say and Say what you Do
- Developing Real Relationships with People

The programme integrates group training and workshop days with one-to-one sessions with either Karen or John. The group days support open dialogue, problem solving and sharing of ideas using practical day to day situations to bring the models and theories to life. The one-to-one sessions then allow the individuals to discover and develop their own strengths and attributes as a leader.

The focus is on practical application and development of these traits for each person in the group based on their skills, needs and goals and linking these to the goals of their organisation.

For more information about the programme and to apply to participate, visit
www.monkeypuzzletraining.co.uk

About the Authors

John McLachlan & Karen Meager

Before they set up Monkey Puzzle Training & Consultancy in 2007, Karen and John both had successful careers in business. Karen worked in the fund management industry in London and John was a chartered accountant in practice and financial director on the board of a number of companies.

Whilst studying for her MBA, Karen became fascinated by the psychological make-up of people who are great at what they do and used her knowledge to recruit and train for all types of roles in her organisation, from call centres to sales to leaders. John had always been more interested in people than accounting and used his warm sense of humour and depth of understanding to help businesses and business owners be successful and live more fulfilling lives. Then they met.

Karen and John are not academics. What they do is take the latest scientific and academic thinking out there and make it usable. They integrate this thinking with their own experience, business understanding and psychological training, make it practical, easy to understand and translate it into something people can do something with. Their goal is that people bring more of themselves to their lives, make their lives easier and be successful in whatever they choose to do.

Recommended Further Reading

Here is a list of books we recommend as supportive reading for this book. They are books we have read, enjoyed and put into practice and they have informed our thinking on many topics in this book.

What Every Parent Needs to Know by Margot Sunderland (ISBN-13: 978-1405320368)

TA Today, A New Introduction to Transactional Analysis by Van Joines and Ian Stewart (ISBN-13: 978-1870244022)

Rewiring your Brain for Love by Marsha Lucas (ASIN: B00DO90W0C)

Thinking, Fast and Slow by Daniel Kahneman (ISBN-13: 978-0141033570)

Healing the Shame that Binds You by John Bradshaw (ISBN-13: 978-0932194862)

The Master and his Emissary by Ian McGilchrist (ISBN-13: 978-0300188370)

Womancode by Alisa Vitti (ISBN-13: 978-1781802007)

Unflappable by Ragini Elizabeth Michaels (ISBN-13: 978-1573244893)

Lightning Source UK Ltd.
Milton Keynes UK
UKOW07f0641111114

241430UK00007B/117/P